Foreword

As we get older many of us become nostalgic for the 'old days' and especially our upbringing. I'm no different. I can't say that Linwood was definitely the best place in the world to be brought up in, but to me it was, and I know from many other Linwoodonians, that they believe so too.

On the 1st of October 2022 I decided to start a new Facebook group called *'Auld Linwood Town & Surrounds'* (ALTS). After getting just six members via invites, I found that its growth was stifled and gave up. This was because of my limited experience of using Facebook and lack of imagination know-how how to grow the group. So, the Facebook group lay dormant until the 06th of February 2023 when I decided to have another go at it. This time I was posting about my own experiences growing up in Linwood and finding out facts about old Linwood from the internet and posting them. The group started to grow as the new members invited their own friends and family. Then in around one month later I subscribed to the online *British Newspapers Archive*, and from there I found that I could find out so much about Linwood going back to when it was born in 1792. With all the new interesting and factual information being posted, the Facebook group took-off and we had 2000 members in less than six months' time. I wisely saved and filed every post that I had made. It is important to say at this point that the group members also helped a lot with their owns facts, but especially their own memories.

I realised that after a few months of what was effectively research - already done, that now more information about Linwood had been gathered than at any time in its history before; much more than had been included in the three books already done on Linwood. Of course, the authors of these books didn't have the luxury of the internet to help the, as the last of these books had been completed in 1999. I then suggested to the group that someone write a book about Linwood, which they could bases on all this data, so much of it being new to everyone. But no one took up the suggestion. Then, on my 59th birthday on the 12th of July 2023, a normal time of reflection, I decided that it had to be me to take on the task of writing the 'Book of Linwood', despite that I'd only ever written *bookies* lines before.

So that's how I got to where I am now.

In this book I've tried to give an extensive account and the timeline of Linwood's history since its beginnings. I've always tried to be as factual as possible and to back-up what I was saying with clear references. This book also includes first-hand accounts of peoples' experiences of Linwood long ago, it is partly anecdotal, and also gives my own experiences of growing up there from the 1960's to the 1980's.

I was born in the Thorn maternity hospital in nearby Elderslie on the 12th of July 1964. Our family had moved to Linwood just a few months before from Govan and lived in the two-apartment at No. 3 Carradale Place. However, as a third child had just come along, they became entitled to three-apartment back-and-front door *Scottish Special Housing Association* (SSHA) house, and so soon we moved to the new house at No. 25 Killin Drive, where I lived until I was eighteen, and my parents until the year 2001, and my brother kept it on until 2006.

It is my hope that this book will inform the people of Linwood, old and young, about its unique history, but also that it be kept as a reference book for people to go to when wanting to know something about Linwood's rich past.

This book is dedicated to the memory of my parents, David and Susan Ross, for bringing Janette, Stewart, and I, to the new promise land that was Linwood. They provided the best upbringing for us and in a wonderful environment, and with wonderful people around us. Without them we would be nothing, and we owe them everything.

Dougie Ross

Index

CHAPTER 1 – IN THE BEGINNING 3
- The Land, the Geology, and the Mineralogy 3
- The Romans 3
- The Middle Ages 4

CHAPTER 2 – FROM THE 18TH CENTURY UNTIL TODAY 5
- Origins 5
- Estates and Neighbouring Hamlets and Villages 6
- Industry 14
- Infrastructure, Services and Amenities 40
- Worship 51
- Education 55
- Transport 59
- Emigration and Culture 61
- The Battle of Linwood Bridge 64
- Environment & Exploration 66
- Health 70
- Crime and Punishment 76
- Living Conditions 78
- The Arts 80
- Community Organisations 82
- Entertainment and Social Activities 84
- Sport 90
- Linwood at War 99
- The Glasgow Invasion & Linwood Expansion 105
- Notable People & Characters 110
- Extraordinary Linwood Stories 114

REFERENCES AND THANKS 117
- References 117
- Thanks 117

CHAPTER 1 – IN THE BEGINNING

The Land, the Geology, and the Mineralogy

The whole area of Linwood had once been under the sea from the beginning until the end of the last Ice Age. Some 14,000 years ago the Ice Age was ending and virtually all the ice in Scotland had melted. This left much of the land area in the Clyde Estuary and the area that much later would become Linwood, flat, silty and sandy. This accounts for the marshland at Linwood Moss and its high-level water table. It may not be surprising therefore, that seashells could be found in the ground all these years later, and this was the case when earth moving equipment got to work when being used in the construction of the *Howwood-Johnstone Bypass* in 1990. The seashells were carbon-dated as being around 25,000 years old when unearthed. Experts explained that melting glaciers had pushed up the sea until low-lying areas stretching from today' Linwood to Irvine, disappeared under the sea, and a section of Renfrewshire became an island. When the waters receded, the shells were buried, until this discovery.

Nearly the whole of the low grounds is alluvial. The subsoil consists chiefly of extensive beds of sand, often interspersed with thin strata of clay, sometimes of moss (peat-bog), and occasionally interrupted with large masses of solid unstratified clay.

Around the mid-19th Century, the district of Linwood was found to be very rich in minerals from the many boreholes taken. This would later give rise to the mining industry in the second half of the 19th Century. These minerals, chiefly Coal, Black and Blue Ironstone, and Shale from which oil could be extracted, were mostly 20-50 fathoms below the surface and so shafts would have to be sank so that they could be mined. Lime was found to be nearer the surface and so open-cast mines would be excavated.

The Romans

Folklore passed down from nearly two millennia ago that tell us about locals hiding behind, as well as up, trees, and of the throwing stones at the occupying Romans. And so it goes that because of this the Romans chopped down all the trees, which led to the creation of Linwood Moss. I find this story fanciful, totally unproven and with no references provided. Yes, authors Rev. John C. Hill and Jim Winters mention these stories in their books about Linwood, but they gave no sources. And it is the same in the other articles and books I've read; there is no evidence provided to back up these claims.

Back then there wasn't even the name *Linwood*, or any of its variant spellings. So, how could a name that didn't even exist be recorded, and by whom? Even the Paisley monks, who were literate, didn't come along until the 15th Century. Only the Romans could write, and there is no evidence that they wrote and recorded anything about Linwood.

And, how can it be that when trees are chopped down, this forms a Moss? No, it doesn't; new trees grow. The Linwood Moss area is marshy and boggy because of the high-water table which remains from the last Ice Age and because the area is very low - just above sea level, and very flat, which is ideal for the formation of bogs, mosses and swamps.

What is true is that the Romans had encampments near Linwood, at Oakshaw in Paisley, at Craigends near Houston, and they built and occupied Barochan Fort.

Barochan Roman Hill Fort

The Romans built a fort on a hill up behind todays Houston Road, and to the west of the old Royal Ordinance Factory - during the reign of Emperor Agricola in AD 69-96.

The remains of a Roman fort are situated on the summit of Barochan Hil, partly in scrubby woodland and partly in arable land. Situated 65m above sea level, it had an approximate size of 80m x 22m. Two pottery fragments recovered from the fort environs bear the stamps of the potters *ALBINVS* and *SVMACI*, both known to have been productive during the Agricolan period, thus giving an approximate date of construction for the fort. A number of bronze *asses* dated to the year 86AD have been uncovered at Barochan. These coins were in almost mint condition, proving that they had been in circulation for only a short period.

First spotted in 1951, where it was noted by OS that the top of this hill had been subjected to artificial steepening and gave the impression of a ditch which was now filled-in, along with a now-levelled bank running around the side of the hill a short distance from the summit.

Aerial photographs revealed it to be a 'Triple Ditched Fort' (which is now divided into four separate fields by a wall running through it). Surrounded by small hillocks and flat pasture lands, this is a peaceful spot. In the late 19th Century, a local farmer moved the Barochan Cross from its original position on the north side of Barochan Burn, to the top of this hill on the South side. Little did he know he was positioning the Celtic Cross on such an ancient site.

The Middle Ages
Very little is known about the lands which now constitute Linwood, between the departure of the Romans and the year 1464 when the area fell into the hands of the monks of Paisley Abbey. They owned 2,000 acres of land in the area, including Lyncleyf [later Linclive], Fulton, Lynwode, Auchans, and owned the rights to fishing the river Black Cart.

Then, by a charter dated the 22nd of March, 1591, these lands passed into the possession of the Abercorn family. However, on the west side of Linwood much of the land around the Clippings area would be owned by the Cochrane family from the 16th Century onwards.

From the book *The Ancestry of Alexander Cochrane*, 1904, we are told *"In 1589, Linwood, a farm in Kilbarchan [Parish], had as a tenant under James Hamilton, first Earl of Abercorn, who possessed it, one William Cochrane."* William Semple, in his continuation of the *History of the Shire of Renfrew*, in 1782, says of Clippings [house] that *"it was the property of John Cochrane, whose ancestors of that name possessed the land for more than three hundred years. He rebuilt the mansion in 1744 with a slate roof and office houses in the form of a court."*

The name *Blackstoun* is noted in 1460 as a grange belonging to Paisley Abbey, the original mansion, and a summer dwelling of the Abbots of Paisley.

The name *Linwood* appears for the first time on a late 16th Century map by *Timothy Pont*.

CHAPTER 2 – FROM THE 18TH CENTURY UNTIL TODAY

Origins

In ascertaining the origins of the name Linwood and its location, we should first look at the word itself. It's had various spellings over the centuries, including *Lynwood, Linnwood, Lynwode,* and *Lenwode*.

So, let's look at the first part of the word, i.e., 'Lin' or 'Linn''. In his book *Linwood, Paisley and District*, of 1953, author Reverend John C. Hill claims that 'Linn' meant 'a deep pool in the wood', but this is the Middle English meaning, whereas it is perhaps more likely that the use of the Scottish Gaelic meaning would apply, i.e., 'Waterfall' or 'Cascade'. Likewise, in his book *Linwood (Images of Scotland)*, of 1999, author James Winters states that Linwood means 'pool in the wood', but does not give a source to back this up.

Next, we look at the second part of the word, i.e., 'wood', or 'wode'. By all accounts this simply means 'wood' as in a treed area.

So, in terms of meaning, the Linwood name derives from 'Waterfall' or 'Cascade' in a wooded area.

So, now we look for the possible location of Linwood's origin. On the eastern edge of Linwood village flows by the river Black Cart. From between the 16th Century and mid-1960's there was a farm called *Linclive Farm* situated about 100m away on the eastern side of the river. The 'Linclive' name also had various changing spellings over the centuries, such as *Linncleave* and *Lincleft*, as indicated on maps, and so we must keep this in mind.

Mr. William Kerr was the Surgeon of Paisley and anonymous correspondent to the *Paisley Herald and Renfrewshire Advertiser* on the 30th of June, and 28th of July, 1866. In his two-part article *Etymons of Paisley Name'*, he gives the following explanation of the origins of Linwood's name and location.

"Linncleave is the bank of the linn; but as Lincleyft is the original form of the word, as is to be found in charters in the Paisley Register, may it not rather signify the rock or crag of the linn? Linncleave is on the Black Cart near Linwood. We presume that rock will be found in the channel of the Cart, there, forming and causing the linn or cascade. "Cliff," The Paisley monks had yare [readied] or fish heck [hell] at Linncleave, in old times, for the taking of salmon''.

In looking at the definitions of 'yare' and 'heck', it could be interpreted as a 'Readied Hell' for the Salmon, i.e., a pool to trap them. And it could be concluded that 'Linclive' (Farm) took it's from the cascading waterfall (Linn) coming from the bank (cliff/cleave/crag), between which there was a salmon [trap] pool, built by the Paisley Monks.

Now, as to the location of the Salmon trap in the river, by a bend, with a bank, in the woods, there is one place where that would likely have been. Today, as was the case hundreds of years ago, there's a bend with a high bank on the Black Cart River at the back of the Public Park, on the left-hand side. It is at bends like this where fish traps were often made, as they are ideal locations for such. Several meters downstream, approaching the two bridges, a weir would have been made of stones (crag or cliff or cleyft), which would enable a pool or dam to form, which would act as a trap for the Salmon, and for the Monks to easily catch them. Immediately after the weir would be a cascade (linn or lyn) of water as it overspilled the weir. This is indicated on the map shown below.

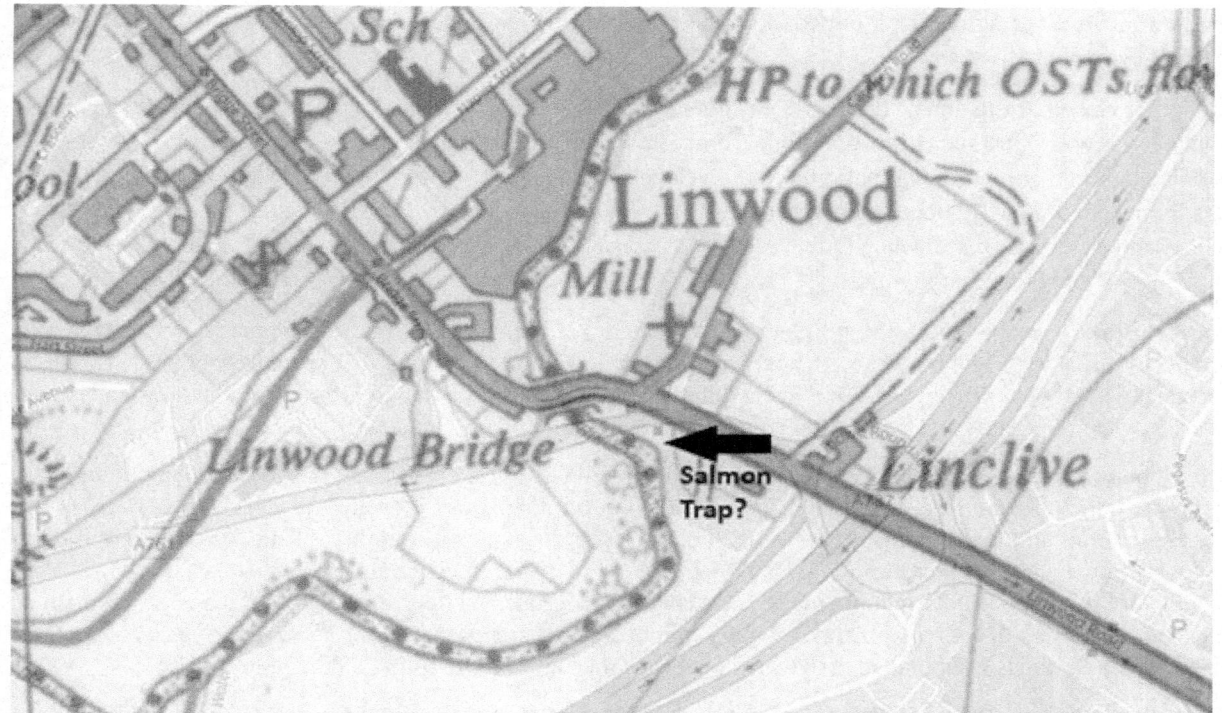

A 1950's map showing Linclive Farm, overlaid with a modern-day map, showing the bend on the River Black Cart, close to Linclive Farm, which is a possible location for the Salmon Trap built by the Paisley Monks several centuries ago, and possibly the source of both the Linwood and Linclive names.

So, the Linwood name was used collectively for an area of farms that were spread quite far part, but there was no village, or even hamlet, in existence until 1792 - with the formation of Cotton Mills and the infrastructure needed around it. This is explained more in the *Industry* section of this book.

The non-existence of Linwood as a place (until 1792) was reflected on in an 'Ecclesiastical Sketch' article published in the *Paisley & Renfrewshire Gazette* on the 13th of January 1877, by the Rev Mr. Carruthers to the Parish Church, the origins of the Johnstone being discussed. The article initially talks about Johnstone's origins on the banks of the river Black Cart and what existed in the area in the year 1780, and then it goes on to say *"A little farther down the water, at the same period, the village now known as Linwood had no existence, the only human habitation there being a farm steading standing about three miles from the cross of Paisley"*. Because we know now where Linwood village was built, being about three miles from Paisley Cross, then we can deduct that the farm steading mentioned was *Linclive Farm*, which had been there near the banks of the river Black Cart since the 16th Century, and long before Linwood Village was created in 1792.

Estates and Neighbouring Hamlets and Villages
Mining Settlements

The small settlements of Inkerman and Balaclava, as well as the area within Linwood village known as Redan Rows, were built to house the workers of the shale coal mines, oil and brickworks in the district of Linwood in the mid-19th century, and all were named after battles in the Crimean War of 1853-56.

Balaclava [later known as Clippens Square], was just south of Clippens House, and was a square of earth-floored cottages and one small licensed convenance shop ran by John Weeple. Its population was 341 in 1871, 948 in 1881, and 699 in 1891, having dropped from its peak in 1881.

Inkerman, near Candrens, had three rows of cottages called Row One, Row Two and Row Three, plus a shop, a school and a schoolhouse. The tiny Hamlet which accommodated the miners and their families was laid out as

Five rows or *raws* of houses with between two and four rooms per house. The lines were called First, Second, Third, Oilwork and Store Rows.

The mines closed at the end of the 19th Century. For a time, a Brickworks operated in Inkerman, making bricks from clay, a waste product from the mining process. By the 1930s the clay was used up, owners Merry and Cunningham had gone into liquidation and the village was put up for sale. When no one bought the village, it was demolished and the population moved to Linwood and Elderslie. What remains of Inkerman is only the School and its House, the Bowling Club, Abercorn Cottage and some pots and scars on the land. Inkerman and Balaclava no longer appear on maps.

Houses in these miners *raws* had no electricity and light was provided by paraffin lamps, water was carried from communal Wells, heating came from coal and peat fires, and toilets were in small freezing 'Privies' in the backdoors. Clothes washing was done in the 'Big Sink' and squeezed through a big cumbersome hand-driven Mangle, with the Iron to smooth out the creases first needing to be heated over the fire.

Shortly before the Second World War, the owner of the mines in the area, *Messrs Merry & Cunninghame Ltd*, went into liquidation and the hamlet of Inkerman was put on the market for sale. The village school was closed forever in 1938 and pupils transferred to Linwood. A short time later, the entire village was demolished and villagers rehoused in Linwood and Elderslie where many of their descendants still live today. Today, the old School, and the famous Inkerman Bowling Club ,which produced many Renfrewshire Champions, still remain as lingering memories of Inkerman's days of glory, although now separated by the A737 Dual Carriageway Spur from the M8 St James Interchange, and which now runs through the site of the old hamlet.

Redan Rows was located on Bridge Street in Linwood. The returning veterans from the Crimean War required homes to live in, and these were duly provided in the forms of basic and small one-storey houses aligned in rows with courtyards between them with water wells. Its population would have no more than 100 at any time as it was much smaller than the other two.

These Miners residencies became known generally as Miners Rows. The state had provided them to house the veterans and their families, adjacent to the coal, shale and ironstone pits, and brickworks (made from shale waste), and oil extraction from shale, where they'd be employed.

Redan Rows was demolished in 1934, Inkerman in 1940, and Clippens Square in 1950.

Aerial photo of Redan Rows, Linwood Village - circa 1933   Store Row, Inkerman – circa early 20th century.

Craigends House and Estate

The *Royal Ordinance Survey Book* [Vol. 14] of 1857, describes the new Craigends House thus. *"Alexander Cunninghame Esquire Prop [Proprietor] Property Plan. Crawfurd's History of Renfrew Valuation Roll. A very excellent and substantially built Mansion House, on the South bank of the "Gryfe", - upwards of 300 years old. The walls of the building, which are very strong are in a perfect state of preservation. In connection with the Mansion are extensive offices and dwelling houses for servants. The whole surrounded by Ornamental grounds and plantations."*

The same document has handwritten notes in red ink that reads as follows.

"Cunninghame of Craigends — This family is lineally descended from William Cunninghame, one or the younger sons of Alexander, first Earl of Glencairn, raised to that dignity by King James III, and who received the lands of Craigends from his father before the end of the 15th century. One of the family, named Gabriel, fell at the battle of Pinkie in 1547. The family is at present represented by a gentleman of the same name."

The mansion was built in 1857 by Mr. Alexander Cunninghame. The Scripture text, with which the front of the building was adorned, were the most outstanding feature of its architectural decoration. The Cunninghame family was one of the oldest in the West of Scotland, and has been connected by marriage with many of the most distinguished houses in Scotland. The estate of Craigends was first granted to William Cunninghame, son of the first Earl of Glencairn, in 1477, so that for 440 years (until 1907), without interruption, a Cunninghame had been at Craigends.

The 15th Century Craigends House was demolished then reconstructed in 1857 to the design of the Architect David Bryce.

A notorious murder took place one dark night in August 1533 on the road from the bridge over the River Gryfe to Craigends House, when William Cunninghame the Laird of Craigends was making his way homewards along the avenue in the company of a servant named John Allanson The pair were virtually within sight of Craigends House when they were ambushed by a wild band of assassins who leaped from the shrubbery and attacked them with daggers and swords The laird and his servant defended themselves resolutely and managed to wound two of their assailants. But they were overpowered by sheer weight of numbers and after a brief bloody conflict both were left lying dead on the avenue. Their shouts for help were drowned by the roar of the River Gryfe raging through the nearby rocky gorge so no one at the mansion knew of their plight until it was too late. Two Semphill servants named Alexander Pinkerton and Thomas Burntshields were both were found guilty of the murders and were subsequently executed.

Members of the Cunninghame family were elected to Parliament for Renfrewshire in 1643 and 1689.

The Cunningham family had sugar plantations worked by slaves in the Jamaica in the Caribbean. By the 1770s, lists of chattels owned by the Cunninghame's give details of nearly 300 enslaved Africans working 377 acres of sugar cane. They were captured on the west coast of Africa and carried in deplorable condition across the Atlantic. When the Cunningham's purchased the Africans off the slave ships, he gave them new names, including 'Kilbarchan', 'Craigends' and 'Paisley'.

By 1834 the Cunninghame's had profited from the Grandville plantation for a century. In the Government compensation records at the abolition of plantation slavery that year, William Cunninghame, 14th laird of Craigends, was awarded £3,278 for the loss of 185 enslaved Africans at Grandville.

Craigends House was damaged by fire in 1951, which destroyed the east wing and caused damage of several thousand pounds. Firemen from Johnstone and Paisley used four jets of water, pumped from the nearby River Gryffe. The part of the house which was destroyed was comparatively small, of single-storey construction, and only contained five rooms. It had been occupied by the Army during the WWII and was unfurnished. The owner at this time was Mrs Allison Cunninghame, an 80-year-old widow, who had left the estate with her sister and four servants, had gone away for a holiday when the fire occurred.

Mr William Cunninghame of Craigends in Houston died on the 09th of August 1993. In past years William had lived in Beith with his wife Helen. They had a daughter called Samantha. The 76-year-old had formerly owned the huge Craigends Estate which included the once famed Craigends House. William Cunninghame was a nephew of the late Mrs Alison Cunninghame, wife of John Charles Cunninghame, the 17th and final laird, who died in 1917. She was the last of the family to live in Craigends House. When she died in November 1958 the estate was inherited by William. Not having the means to maintain the estate, however, the estate was left derelict and, after a few years, sold to the housing construction company Taylor Woodrow. The estate and mansion house were left abandoned for many years and fell into extreme dilapidation. In 1971 the mansion house was part-demolished and by 1973, Taylor Woodrow had started construction on the first of what would be many housing estates within the grounds. The final remaining entrance tower of the building was demolished in 1980, and almost all of the estate would be occupied by new housing over the next two decades.

Designed and Bulit in 1857 by Architect David Bryce: Watercolour perspective of main elevation of Craigends House at that time.

Alison Cunninghame of Craigends (née Pearson) with her sister, Laura – circa 1909.

Linwood boy Austin Donnelly (aged 6) outside Craigends House in 1970 – one year before its tragic demolition by Taylor-Woodrow housebuilders.

The Craigends Lion, the only part of house that remains. Now situated at Carrick Centre, Houston

Burnbrae House and Estate

Burnbrae House was said to be one of the most beautiful mansions in Renfrewshire. It was built in the Gothic style with a turreted roof, stone carved balustrades, pillared porches, bay windows and balconies, and set in idyllic rural surroundings with farmland, woodland and beautiful gardens. It had been in the Speirs' family since the early 18th Century, with farming being the main income. However, the three sons of Robert Spier, the third Laird of Burnbrae, William and twin brothers Thomas and Robert had decided that India was the place to make their fortunes. William went into business in India as a partner in Grove, Spier and Company while his two brothers first formed a Glasgow manufacturing firm R & T Spier, which had been involved with a successful London company who was heavily involved with the East Indies. In India Robert had a silk print factory and Thomas a dyeing factory, both very successful.

In about 1838 the brothers returned to Britain wealthy men with William settling in Brighton, and Robert and Thomas returning to Burnbrae, whereupon William Napier sold Blackstoun Estate, including Blackstoun House, to Thomas Spier in 1847.

It was at Burnbrae where in 1839 Robert married Mary daughter of Sir William Milliken Napier of Milliken. Robert succeeded to Burnbrae on the death of his father two years later but in 1842 purchased the Culdees Estate near Crieff Perthshire.

Robert Spier died in 1853 at Burnbrae which was put in the trust of his brother Thomas. Not a man to be idle Thomas Spier opened a Mineral Quarry and Works at Linwood and had 40 acres of bog at what was previously 'Blackstoun Moss', reclaimed it for farming.

Thomas Spier made more wealth when he collaborated with a coalmaster from Airdrie called William Black and his associates, by giving them the lease of the Blackstone estate, and set about sinking a went on to mine coal, ironstone and shale. Together they formed the Blackstoun Mineral Oil Company.

Thomas lived with his sister and nephew at Burnbrae House, and they had a footman, butler, and four female servant who attended to their needs.

Thomas Spier died in 1874 the Blackstoun Estate was inherited by his nephew Robert Thomas Napier Spier, his brother Roberts only son, who then inherited Burnbrae House upon reaching adulthood in 1860, and then decided to live at the Spiers' Culdees House in Perthshire. The Spier family connection with Burnbrae House ended in 1886 with the death of Thomas Spier's sister, Agnes Spier. Burnbrae House passed through several more owners before being sold, and the house was demolished in 1940.

In the 1960's the pressed steel plant and the car factory at Linwood were built on the area, and today the area is occupied by the Malcolm Group haulage company.

Blackstoun House and Estate

The original mansion, a summer dwelling of the Abbots of Paisley, was a house was built by George Shaw in the latter part of the fifteenth century as the ancestral home of the Napier family and the Laird of Blackstoun. After the Reformation, the house was improved by James, Earl of Abercorn. It was later down burned down about 1730 and then Alexander Napier had it rebuilt.

Folklore tells us that Blackstoun House was looted by the Jacobites during the 1745 uprising and that Bonnie Prince Charlie rounded-up horses in the Linwood Moss woods for his. Jacobite army.

The Blackstoun Estate consisted of, at various periods, the Mansion House, Blackstoun Mill, Blackstoun Holm Farm, Blackstoun Mains Farm, Blackstone Mineral Works, Blackstoun Oil Works, Blackstoun Lodge, Brickwork Rows for the workers, and a school for the workers children. The Mill was of four storeys, with a Storehouse of two storeys, and a Gate-House.

Paisley Herald and Renfrewshire Advertiser advertised the whole of Blackstoun Estate for sale on the 19th of August 1865. The advert explained that *"The Property was for some years occupied by the late Mr. James Henderson as a Cotton Mill, and thereafter by Messrs. Patterson & Neilson, and others, as a Print Work. It is well adapted for either description of Public Work, or could easily converted into Weaving Factory. There an abundant supply of water from the River Black Cart brought into the Work"*.

There was also a Machine Gun and Magazine site near the Brickwork Rows in the early part of the 20th century, presumably a defensive mechanism during WWI.

In the case of the Blackstoun Mineral Works, Linwood people growing up in second half of the 20th century would know this as the 'Red Rocks', a place full of pools of water and red coloured rocks, where frogs, frogspawn, tadpoles and newts could be found.

In the year 1843 the Napier family sold the Blackstoun Estate to Thomas Spier of nearby Burnbrae House. Blackstoun House was demolished in 1939.

Merchiston House

Major James Milliken, who made his fortune from West Indian sugar and tobacco plantations, purchased the Merchiston Estate from the Houstoun family in 1733.

Merchiston House was a four-storey Georgian mansion, shady woodlands, orchards, manicured lawns, terraced gardens, dovecotes, ornamental statues, walled ditches, trimmed hedges, waterfalls and ponds, was acquired by his great-grandson, Colonel Robert Napier, whose relatives owned Blackstoun House. The family was related to the renowned mathematician John Napier (1550-1617), of Merchiston Castle, Edinburgh, who invented logarithms.

Several ironstone mines nearby providing Merchiston estates with much of their wealth, and although Merchiston House was demolished in 2008, today in the adjacent woodland, black muddy water still seeps out of the ground from the long-abandoned quarries.

In 1998 the village of Brookfield was created near Merchiston House, at the other side of the woods.

Merchiston was commandeered as a military hospital during wartime. Patients included soldiers wounded on European battlefields.

Merchiston House later became a mental health facility and was managed by NHS Greater Glasgow and Clyde. It had been commissioned as a replacement for Broadfield Hospital at Port Glasgow and was established by converting the 19th century building in 1948. Two new wings were added in 1958. Modern facilities were created on the site in 1984 and the mansion was subsequently demolished after services had been transferred to the Southern General Hospital, Merchiston Hospital closed in 2008. The other estate buildings were demolished in 2013 in order to better secure the site. It is likely that Merchiston Avenue in Linwood is named after it.

Clippens House

The current Clippens House, on Clippens Road, has been rebuilt in 1817 by Peter Cochrane, by the Cochrane family, which owned much of the land around Linwood during the 16th century. The Clippens name was formerly Clippings, and is thought to be derived from the time when the monks of Paisley Abbey allowed the local people to cut or clip the surrounding fields.

This Georgian country mansion consisted of a Room, Double Drawing-Room, Billiard Room, 8 Bedrooms (3 With Dressing-Rooms), 3 Bathrooms and Lavatories, Kitchen, Pantry, Wine Cellar, Servants' Hall and 3 Bedrooms, Laundry, and other Extensive Accommodation. There was also a Gardener's House or Lodge, Coachman's House, Stable (4 Stalls and 2 Loose Boxes), Coach-House, Harness Room, Washhouse, etc. The Grounds, were well enclosed and in fine order, extended to about 55 Acres, and include Flower and Kitchen Garden (with Greenhouse and small Fernery), Lawns and Park.

Peter Cochrane made his fortune in India where he lived from 1774 until 1817. He remained at Clippens until his death in 1831 when it was inherited by his son who died childless in 1835. There then followed a wrangle lasting 25 years which made legal history with claimants coming forward from all directions before a Hugh Ferrier of Puerto Rico was legitimised as the rightful heir.

The emergence of the shale and oil industry in the Clippens vicinity helped to make the ancestral estate of the Cochranes even more valuable and because so many people were employed locally in this work four rows of houses and a small village school were set up at Clippens, and was named Balaclava.

Local stories tell of the house being haunted, with ghostly figures resembling cavaliers clad in flowing robes, and wearing feathered hats and thigh-length boots have been seen in the neighbourhood, as well as the sound of horse's clip-clopping about the empty courtyard. Over the years locals also told of mysterious shrouded figures digging up corpses from the ground and of floating hands hovering above people sleeping in some of the modern houses nearby. There was also a report that at least one family living in the Clippens vicinity, Abernethy Drive, moved house because of the spectral apparitions and that other local residents experience uncanny feelings of uneasiness as they pass the old house at night.

From the 1960s until the early 1980s, during the *Cold War*, the house was used as the Civil Defence Emergency Planning Centre for Renfrewshire, which included a Nuclear Bunker. Renfrew District Council then used the building for offices. Having lain abandoned for a time, the house was put up for sale in 1989 and the redeveloped as flats in 1993, as part of the *Lindon Gate* development.

Linwood House

Linwood House on Napier Street was built around the time of the Cotton Mill opening in 1792, it was purchased by one of the Mill co-owners Mr James Brown in 1802 after the Cotton Mill [re-built in 1805] had been burnt down causing financial losses to the firm. It was located half-way along the road where Napier Gardens is today.

This blonde sandstone villa consisted of 3 Public Rooms, 5 Bedrooms, 2 Dressing Rooms, and accommodation for Servants. It also had Office Houses consisting of Coach-House, a Three-Stalled Stable and Harness Room, Washing-House and Laundry, Dog Kennel and Greenhouse. There was also a Large Kitchen and Fruit Garden. The Grounds extended to about 3 Acres.

Various titled people and businessmen occupied the house over its lifetime until it was finally demolished in 1970's after the last residents, the Hick family, who owned a bus firm, left it.

Georgetown

Just outside Linwood, adjacent to the end of Moss Road, Netherfield Cottages, the houses of Georgetown village were situated on the B790 Houston Road between Inchinnan and Houston, until the early 1950's. They were constructed in 1915 to house workers at the No.4 Shell Filling Factory [Royal Ordinance Factory], in order to assist in the WWI effort. It was the job of the workers, 15:1 women-to-men ratio, to fill the artillery shells with explosives ready to be shipped out to the front.

Georgetown village had a population of around 400 people at its peak and consisted of a multi-use Village Hall/Cinema/Church, a number of wooden cottages, a Sub Post Office, and a Railway Station. The factory and village were named after the Prime Minister David Lloyd George after he paid a visit to the factory in 1915.

The *Scotsman* reported on the 24th of April 1918 that the munitions workers at the Georgetown factory had presented a battle-plane to the RAF as an indication of their warm regard for the members of the fighting forces and their whole-hearted effort to assist by money, as well as by hard work, for the nation in these anxious days. They each contributed sums varying from 2s. 6d. to 7s. 6d. a week, and organised a fancy-fair, concerts , cinema entertainments, and a fancy-dress ball to raise the funds. The sum aimed at was over-subscribed. The idea originated among the workers themselves, and the gift was quite apart from their usual investments in War Bonds. Mr Churchill, Minister of Munitions, asked the general manager of the factory to convey to the workers his sincere appreciation of their patriotic action in presenting the battle-plane .

After WWI ended in 1918, and so the need for shells, most of the population was moved largely to Inchinnan and Houston, although the post office lasted until 1939, the Railway Station until 1959, and some of houses nearer the Railway station lasted until the early 1970's before all being demolished. Today there are still traces of the foundations, the railway and station to be seen at the road side.

Linwood Camp

Linwood Camp was situated on the Paisley side of Linwood Road, roughly behind the corner where the McDonalds fast food restaurant is today. It was built just after WWII between 1945-46 and would be demolished by 1953.

Linwood Camp was one of many similar such temporary camps. The Sunday post reported on the 18th of August 1946 that there were already twelve Army camps and one Italian P.O.W. camp taken over by homeless families in the West of Scotland.

The camp was made up of numbered Nissan huts which had originally been used by the army and then as an Italian P.O.W. camp, but by 1946 homeless families moved into the huts. The new residents [referred to as 'squatters'] made themselves busy getting their new homes ship-shape, laying carpets and linos on concrete floors and partitioning huts into rooms. The majority of squatters were ex-Servicemen, who declared — *"They'll need an army to put us out."*

Tradesmen then started to call with milk and provisions, the police were holding a watching brief, a water supply was connected, and health officials tended to sanitation. However, electricity hadn't yet been supplied even though the huts are wired. Coal and dross left by the Forces were being used in the stores. Meetings were held at the camps to elect leaders.

In reading over newspaper archives of the time about the occurrences in, or related to Linwood Camp, it clear to me that there was a high rate of crime committed by the residents. It is not clear how they had become homeless, with the men of the families coming back from the war, but it seems many of the unfortunates had been through hard times. But in any case, many were unruly and were apt to drunkenness, fighting and theft. Below are some examples of such misdemeanours.

The *Paisley Daily Express* reported on Friday the 21st of March 1952, that a 22-year-old woman had been sent to prison for 30 days for neglecting here 4 children, aged between 2 months and 4 years. It was reported that she *"failed to provide them with adequate clothing and bedding and by keeping them in a dirty and verminous condition"*. It had been found that she hadn't done these things deliberately, but rather it was due to her husband having deserted her and her intellectual incapacity, i.e., *"too ignorant or too stupid"*. Nevertheless, and sadly, the children were removed to a home *"where they would be properly cared for"*. The poor woman *"left the dock sobbing bitterly."*

From the PDE on Friday the 03rd of August 1951, was reported the story of a 26-year-old man who went to jail for 7 days due to beating his wife black and blue by *"striking her several blows on the face and body with his fists"*. In his defence he had said that *"he and his wife had been had been arguing because they had no place to stay"*.

Also reported in the *Paisley Daily Express* on Saturday the 15th of September 1951, a constable on a Linwood bound bus noticed two men acting suspiciously and throwing to sacks under a bus stairway. Once the men got off the bus at Linwood Camp the constable followed them and stopped them. The two men aged 30 (labourer) and 23 (textile worker) were then taken to Linwood Police Station where the sacks were found to contain 1 ½ ctws of Lead with a value of £10 10s. The men later appeared in court and claimed that they had bought the Lead from a man. They were then given the option of a fine or imprisonment.

Linwood House was built around the time of the Cotton Mill opening in 1792 and soon occupied by Mill co-owner Mr James Brown in 1802. It was demolished in the 1970's.

Clippens House was rebuilt in 1817 by Peter Cochrane. It was later used by the Civil Defence Emergency Planning Centre from 1960's to 1980's. It was converted to flats in 1993.

Merchiston House was built in the 19th century. It was acquired by Robert Napier. It became an NHS mental health facility in 1948 and was demolished in 2008.

Blackstoun House was originally built in the 15th century, burnt down and rebuilt in the 1730's. It was the Napier family ancestral home. It was demolished in 1939.

Burnbrae House was built in the early 18th century. It was originally owned by William Napier and sold to Thomas Spier in 1847. It was then demolished in 1940.

Netherfield Cottages at Georgetown village on Houston Road. Built in 1915 to house workers at the No.4 Shell Filling Factory to assist in the WW1 effort, and demolished in the 1950's.

Industry

In this chapter we go through the industries in order that made Linwood, beginning with farming as the Linwood area started out as just a collection of small farms which lasted hundreds of years. The first Industrial Revolution changed this with the arrival of the Cotton Mill, and the second Industrial Revolution brought the Mining, the Paper Mill, and Engineering. Later in the mid-20th century came the Car Factory came, lasted just 18 years, and then traditional industries gradually disappeared going into the 21st century.

Farming

Many of the farms in Linwood and surrounding areas, namely: Mill O'Cart, Farm of Green, Muirhead, Home Farm, Blackstoun Home Rywraes, Clippens, East and West Fulton, Nether Mains, Anderson, Nether Craigends, Fulwood, Auchens, Netherfield, Selvieland, Birkenhead, Muirhead, West Candren, Barskiven, Middleton, and Linclive, date back to at least the 16th century and are indicated on the *Timothy Pont* (1583-1614) map from that period, albeit with differences in spelling. Some of these still exist today, while others were still in existence until the early 1960's when the expansion of Linwood put paid to some of them. Below is an overview of some of them.

This grainy aerial photo of the Mill O'Cart farm was taken in 1963, The farm dates back to at least the 16th century, and possibly longer ago. The Lade can be seem running along the front of the farm, as can the dirt track at the end of Clippens Road – leading to the *Shoogley* bridge over the river Black Cart. And just sneaking into the picture is the roof of one of the houses in the new Kintyre housing scheme.

Linclive Farm

Probably the oldest know farm in the Linwood area, dating back to the 15th century at least. Linclive has also been known as Lincleave and Lincleyft over the centuries.

The name in todays' parlance effectively means 'bank of the linn', with 'linn' in Scots' language meaning cascade or waterfall. The 'clive' part derives from ancient words 'clivus' or 'cleft' that later evolved to 'cliff', which we would today call embankment or just bank.

Just 100m or so from where the farm was located, lies the bend (with a high bank) in the river Black Cart where it is thought that the Paisley Monks built a Salmon Trap, which would have been in the form of dam to trap the fish, and the dam wall would have water overspilling form it and cascading downstream. And so, we have not only the likely origin of the name Linwood, but the likely location.

Linclive was farmed up to the mid 1960's when it was demolished to make way for what became the Linclive Link Road and Roundabout.

East Fulton Farm

Also known as Low Fulton in the 19th century, East Fulton Farm, on Darluith Road, or as late 20th century Linwoodonians knew it 'Stirling Farm', because of the Dairy Farm milk supply business ran from there by Allan

Stirling, but in fact had been called East Fulton for hundreds of years. It has been there since the 15th century and took the original form of its name from the word 'Fauldubs', or 'Fold-town', meaning 'the farm house near the fold, or enclosure for Animals'. It also is shown on maps as far back as the 1500's as 'Foulton'.

Its age, along with that of neighbouring West Fulton Farm, must make them the oldest [still standing] inhabited dwellings in the Linwood area, although it's not clear if it has ever been rebuilt or added to.

No longer a farm, it is today called 'Stirling Powersports' and supplies Motorbikes, Sports Boats, Quad Bikes, etc, since 1995.

West Fulton Farm

Also known as High Fulton in the 19th century, West Fulton is situated on Fulton Drive, and thought to be as old as East Fulton Farm nearby, although It's not clear if it has ever been rebuilt or added to.

As well as it being a farm, there was a Blacksmiths workshop situated there in the 19th century, as there is today.

Market Garden

Erskinefaulds (aka Erskine Falls), was situated around the middle of where Vernon Drive is today. The Cart Track leading up to it, was from the top of today's Blackwood Avenue.

The 1856-7 Voters Roll states *"A small cottage with garden attached. Occupier William Gray. The property of Hugh Ferrier, Esquire"*, and in the 1901 *Watson's Paisley & District Directory* it states *"William Wilson, Market Gardener, Erskine Faulds."*

It was demolished in the early 1960's to make way for the new housing scheme of Stirling Drive catchment area.

Farm of Green

Dating back to the late 17th century, it was known as the 'Farm of the Green' until the 20th century, when it became 'Green Farm', which todays' road adjacent to where it stood, was named after.

During the 19th century they regularly advertised their produce in newspapers which consisted of usual farm crop vegetables grown on 114 ½ acres of arable land, as well as manure, lime and coal.

George Craig was the last owner of it, then it was demolished in the 1960's, and the new St Conval's Church built on that land in 1967.

Middleton Farm

Middleton farm has been where it is today since the 15th century at least and there still exists an ancient ruin beside the farm buildings.

In September 1999 there was a fatal plane crash nearby which was first spotted by one on Middleton farm's labourers, who pulled some of the occupants free.

Today the farm is used by the firm 'Mitchell Turf', who supply turf for lawns.

East Fulton Farm building – Circa 1970's

West Fulton Farm building – Circa 2023

Farm or Green (Green Farm) – Circa 1950.

Middleton Farm – Circa 2022

Clippens Farm

Clippens Farm served as the Home Farm for the Clippens Estate. It was later owned by the Renfrew County Council who let it as a Tenancy Farm. John Stirling and his family of eight lived in it from the 1930's and his son Allan and new wife Mary lived there for a short while before moving to East Fulton Farm to run the Allan Stirling Dairy Farm. Clippens Farm was last farmed in the 1960's and the Council then converted it into a depot for their parks department. The Clippens Villa was occupied until the 1980's before demolition.

Clippens Villa shown at the top, Clippens Farm in the middle, and Rywraes Farm building at the bottom. Circa 1963. The new Montrose Place and Athol Place are just visible on the right of the picture off Brediland Road.

Tomato Houses (Nurseries)

The *Paisley Daily Express* reported on the 16th of February, 1911, of a proposal made by *Messrs J. and C. Gilchrist, Arthur's Crag, - Lanark*, applying for a supply of water for tomato houses proposed to be erected by them at Linwood. They further stated that if the Council would lay the necessary water pipe from Linwood to the Old Toll House, that they would guarantee a return of 10% on the Council's outlay for a period of ten years. The council's Mr Lee informed the committee that the probable cost of laying the pipe would be £100, and so after consideration it was agreed to lay the pipe subject to the proposed guarantee.

And soon after in 1911, with a water supply installed, the Tomato Houses, or Nurseries, were born, just off Middleton Road, and was considered by locals at the time as Linwood's own "Crystal Palace" with five acres of glasshouses for growing tomatoes.

The business lasted until sometime in the 1960's and by the 1970's the Nursery Cottages were demolished and land returned to more regular crops farming.

The Tomato Nurseries and Cottages – circa 1933, Consisted of five acres of glasshouses for growing tomatoes.

Cotton Industry

In the late 18th century, the cotton industry was booming and mills were already established in the English Midlands and in Lancashire. A group of wealthy businessmen, local to the farming area collectively known as Linwood, saw the opportunity to open up their own Cotton Mill on the banks of the River Black Cart. They were: Mr Shanks, Grandfather to Ex-Provost Shanks of Johnstone; Mr William Napier, who afterwards became the Laird of Blackstoun, and Mr James Dunlop.

It's likely these men sought the advice of Civil Engineers and subsequently picked this ideal location to take advantage of the meandering curve in the river whereby they could create a dam with a weir upriver, then cut an almost straight, but dog-legged Lade, to their mill coming from the sluice gates at the dam, and another about half-way along at the corner of the dog-leg, to feed the mill then discharge the used water back into the river downstream where it returned from its curve. The revolving water wheels were devised by Civil Engineer Sir William Fairbairn, who had designed hundreds of bridges across Britain, including one over the Menai Straits between North Wales and Anglesey.

With funds secured, the building of the mill began and was for the most part completed when it opened for production in 1792. As well as the mill necessary infrastructure had to be put in-place and this was done in the building of two new streets perpendicular to the mill, with houses and amenities to support the workers and the business. One street was named Napier Street after the co-owner William Napier, and the second one was named Bridge Street after the Linwood Bridge spanning the River Black Cart, which had been built in 1776 by the Cochranes'.

One account of the time described the status of the new village shortly after its opening, as follows.

"The building is already finished except one wing, which yet remains to be added. The house is six storeys with garrets. It already contains 400 glass windows, and when completed will contain 540. The depth of fall [meaning water supply which was brought the Cart from short distance below Johnstone] is 17 feet. The tide makes, up to the tail of the wheel, but when interrupted by tail water they have another wheel, more elevated, which they can put in motion."

It seems that the Manager, Mr. Dunlop, paid very laudable attention to the health, safety, welfare, and ergonomics of the workers in the construction of the mill building. He assured that the certain features were designed-in, so that roofs of rooms were high, the machinery much simplified in their manufacture and could easily cleaned, and that there was little or no waste, or particles of cotton to fly about, and a large space allowed in proportion to the machinery; the consequence of which, fewer workers would be crowded into the same space. In addition, the whole apparatus did not take above three half-gills of oil daily; hence no bad would arise from the oil. Add to all that the fact that the whole building was subdivided by two vast staircases, which acted ventilators.

One local Minister looked out for the welfare of the children when he said *"If equal attention is paid to the instruction of the children, I should consider at a work of this sort, a school where children of the poor, otherwise a burden upon their parents, may be trained to industry and virtue."* Of course, child labour wasn't so frowned upon then, but at least he provided them with a half-day school education in Napier Street, and the chance to earn some money for their families. So at least they weren't working all day.

In the 18th Century British companies procured their cotton chiefly from Egypt, the West Indies and India, the process being easier from the latter two mentioned due to them being colonies and part of the 'Great' British Empire. The sources changed going into the 19th Century when better quality American cotton came onto the market and it could be shipped quickly and straight to nearby Glasgow.

Because of the sources of Great Britain, and Linwood's cotton, it could be claimed that Linwood was a village founded on slavery. This may not be strictly true in the case of when Egypt was the source of Cotton, but in the cases of the workers who picked cotton in British West Indies and India, they were certainly slaves of the British Empire, and later in cotton fields in the USA, specifically the states of Georgia, Alabama, Mississippi, and Louisiana; the workers were slaves of what became the Confederate South. So, in essence, there would have been no Linwood without the cotton that was purchased at cheap prices due to the pittance of wages paid, if indeed there were any wages paid to the native populations of the aforementioned countries. Such a lucrative business would not have been feasible without slavery. So, you best make your own mind up.

On Monday the 27th of April 1795, an advert was placed in the *Caledonian Mercury*, the sale of 'A Cotton Mill and Machinery', along with five acres of land and two large houses. It is not known why they tried to sell the business so soon after opening just three years before.

The mill was at its peak of production in 1800, but in 1802 it burnt down as the result of an accident. It was however, rebuilt, and opened again in 1805. Sometime after it was rebuilt it contained a total of 28,000 spindles, which 400 workers operated, and that the wages every Saturday amounted to a total of £190. Some 1800 workers would be employed at the mill at its zenith.

The breakdown of the wages in the mills early days was thus. Eighty workers received from 16s. to 30s. per week, two hundred from 6s. to 13s., and one hundred and twenty from 3s. to 6s. There was among the workers, even that time the early part of the present century — a benefit society into which 3d. a week was paid, and out of which 6s. a week was received members when unfit for work and 8s when confined to bed.

The first change in ownership was about 1820, when Mr. Andrew Brown is mentioned proprietor the mill. Mr. Brown died about 1856, but for a time previous to this had been partnered in business by his cousin Mr James Brown, of Linwood House, who continued the management of the mill till his death in 1859. He was succeeded in the proprietorship of the business by Mr. John Napier Milliken, son-in-law Mr. Andrew Brown, (who, with his wife, resided in Merchiston House, erected for the latter by her father). Mr. Napier carried on the Linwood Mill till 1862, when his connection with the latter ceased. The Linwood Mill remained in his possession till seven years later, in 1869, when it was for the sum of £15,000 to a Mr Ronaldson, who retained possession of the mill till 1879, his connection with it thus extending over a period of ten years, and this period, may be mentioned, was one of the most, if not the most, successful in its history. During it, many alterations were made on the premises, extensive addition was executed, in the shape of the "new mill." These ten years constituted, indeed, the palmy days of cotton-spinning in Linwood.

When Mr Ronaldson sold the mill in 1879 to Mr G. W. Richardson, of Ralston, for £16,000, he only made a profit of £1000 over his purchase-money, though during his tenure of management large additions had been made to the buildings. During Mr. Richardson's proprietorship, the business was carried on under title of Storer and Sons. Messrs Storer of Thorn, whose Elderslie mill had recently been burned, having joined Mr. Richardson in the management. However, the partnership was dissolved on the 11th of November 1880 – by mutual consent, as reported in the *Edinburgh Gazette*. In 1888 the concern passed into hands of a limited liability company, which, till the winding-up of the business in December 1893, held possession of the mill, trading under the name of the *Linwood Cotton Spinning Company Ltd*. The Directors of this company were mostly English manufacturers, who had extensive connection with the cottons spinning trade in Glasgow and the English manufacturing centres. Though the mill has passed through the hands of proprietors, there have been but few managers connected with it, these being far known Mr. Joseph Watt and Mr. Alex. Watt, the former from 1805 and the latter till; Mr. Alex. Malloch from 1848 till Mr. John Gibson from 1879 till 1882; and Mr. Andrew Faulds from till the close of the mill.

Mr Andrew Faulds took a lively interest in the affairs the village, and was much respected the workers; and it was in February 1893 that he received handsome presentation on his leaving the village to fill-in the in an Ayrshire mill.

So why did the Cotton Mil business close after so many years of successful trade? Put simply, the mill was closed because it had become a non-profit-earning concern, through keen competition. The American Civil of 1861-65 was the main reason for the eventual demise of many mills, and this created the "cotton famine" from 1862, which quickly transformed the global economy. The price of cotton soared from 10 cents a pound in 1860 to $1.89 a pound in 1863-1864. Britain then turned to other countries that could supply cotton, such as India, Egypt, and Brazil, but costs were higher.

In April 1863 a *Cotton Districts Distress Relief Fund* was set up by the County of Renfrew and a sub-committee met to consider applications for relief from districts in Renfrewshire suffering from the cotton failure. The sub-committee agreed to provide grants to Linwood, Lochwinnoch, and Bridge of Weir. They had at that point, already expended £600 for relief of distress in the county.

New buildings, new plant, and magnificent railways and steamboat connections in Glasgow, Manchester, and others great British cities, had in the latter years of the Linwood mills, rendered it almost impossible to carry on a successful business in a building of limited accommodation and with somewhat antiquated machinery. In older days when prices, owing to the absence of keen competition, were better, the Linwood mill could return good profits, without even so much a railway within miles of the village, and when all the raw material and the goods manufactured had to be carted from and to Glasgow. At that time Linwood yarn, owing to its superior manufacture, commanded best prices in the market.

Linwood Cotton Mill, established in 1972, and was the largest in the UK. Burnt down in 1802, rebuilt by 1805.

Calico Printing Machine in operation in the 19th century.

Henderson's Cotton Mill

Mr J. Henderson was the proprietor of the Mill, which was Linwood's second cotton mill and built shortly after the big mill next door to it, but with only a tenth of the big mill's 400 workers at that period. It was in this Mill building that *Messrs R. & W. Watson* initially set up their Paper Mill a century later.

Calico Shawl Printing

Calico was a heavy plain-woven textile made from unbleached, and often not fully processed cotton. This kind of cotton Linwood procured from India; America did not produce cotton until well into the 1800's.

Mr J. Henderson was the proprietor of the Linwood Calico Printworks, which printed patterns, including the world-famous *Paisley Pattern*, on shawls supplied by the Paisley Mills. Patterson and Neilson were owners and went bankrupt in 1954. Later owners *Messrs Daniel Crawford and Son* also went bankrupt in 1859.

Bleaching Cotton Fabric

Beside the big cotton mill there was also a small thread bleachfield. Further down the river at Middleton there was a much bigger thread bleachfield, started by James Smith by 1782. Bleaching at the time involved a sequence of repeated steepings in water, boiling in lye, soaping, soaking in buttermilk (then into the 19th century in diluted sulphuric acid) – together with extensive "grassing" – spreading the fabrics out in the sun in "bleachfields" for periods of weeks. Later bleaching would be done indoors.

Mining & Heavy Engineering Industries

Fulwood Tile Works

Situated at end of Moss Road, on the left and just before Fulwood Bridge. These works where in operation around the mid-19th century period and the tiles manufactured were chiefly used for drainage purposes. It consisted of a shack, with two kilns, and a portion of waste ground attached.

Mining

Minerals mined in the Linwood area were Coal, Lime, Shale, Coal-Shale, and Ironstones of the Black & Blue band varieties, the latter two being from a group of iron-rich sedimentary rocks that can smelted to create iron and products made from iron. Coal was used for heating and cooking, but also for the processing of Limestone in Kilns, and the Limestone itself mainly for improving the soil in farming. Shale had its oil content extracted from it.

The owners of the mines in the Linwood, Clippens, Inkerman, and Blackstoun, were: *Merry & Cunninghame, James Dunlop and Co., James Anderson, J. Liddell and Co., Allan Craig and Sons*, the former being by far the owner of the greatest number of pits, and so the biggest employer in the mining industry in the area, them also owning the Clippens Oil Company. There would have been several hundred employed locally by these companies. Of course, the local landowners such the *Speirs* of Elderslie and Burnbrae House, and the *Napiers* of Merchiston House, would receive royalties for their land being worked and exploited.

As a rule, the sons of miners followed the occupation of their fathers, and began to work when they reach twelve years of age—by which time they were now fairly proficient in reading, writing, and arithmetic. After they commenced to work, however, they were encouraged to make further progress in education, and for that purpose evening classes were taught at most of the schools.

The average wage at the pits in the late 19th Century was 4s. 6d. a-day per week, although what a miner got for his labour could not always be stated in shillings and pence, however, as he sometime enjoyed special advantages in the way of a free house, cheap education for his children, and the like. Thus, the average take-home wage was 3s. 6d. a-day.

When a boy of twelve years entered a pit, he was attached to his father or some other man, and became what was known technically as a "*quarter-man*." At fourteen, the boy became a *half-man* at sixteen, a *three-quarter-man*, and at eighteen, he assumed the title of miner, performed a man's work, and drew a man's pay. When the boy ranked as a *quarter-man* he usually received 1s. a-day; when a *half-man*, 2s.; and when a *three-quarter-man* 3s a day.

Danger was never far away in the pits. Mine faces and roof-arches could collapse causing men to be crushed, the build-up of noxious and inflammable gases could cause asphyxiation, explosion and burns from fires, and in many cases proving fatal.

Linwood had become quiet and still, with many men unemployed. However, evidence of past prosperity and undeveloped greatness could still be seen. Black mountains of slate and waste reared themselves on either side of the low-lying village, standing out clear and distinct for miles around as ugly landmark, and occasionally the trundling of coal trucks from some still busy mine disturbed the silence which prevailed.

With the exception of the Walkinshaw No. 2 Pit that closed in 1915, the mining industry lasted just a few short decades in the Linwood area, from the 1850's until the 1890's. During that period there were between 12-18 pits generally going at one time.

Clippens Shale Oil Works

The *Clippens Oil Works* were built in 1870 by the *Clippens Shale Oil Company*; a co-partnership of Robert Binning, John Binning, and Thomas Inglis Scott. After financial problems and court case, the business was carried forward by James Scott, father of Thomas Inglis Scott, who then promoted The *Clippens Oil Company Ltd* in 1878. In 1876 the oil company took over mines in the area from *Messrs. Merry & Cunninghame*, until that date, supplies of shale were purchased from that company.

The *Clippens Shale Oil Company Limited* was part of *Pentland Oil Works*, Loanhead, Edinburgh. Their aims were *"The leasing and acquiring of shale, coal, fireclay and other minerals, and limestone, clay and raw or impurified oil and other materials, and searching for, working, raising and manufacturing the same into oil, and paraffin and other products. The selling and disposing of the said shale and other minerals and materials and the products thereof, and the purchasing and dealing therein, and in other materials and products and carrying on the business of oil manufacturers and merchants"*.

An article in the *North British Daily Mail* on the 03rd of April 1878, in regard to the operations growth since its inception, suggested that *"since that time they have gradually extended in size till now they are perhaps the second largest of their kind in the world."*

The *North British Daily Mail* reported on the 30th of April 1873 on the trade prospects of the *Clippens Shale-Oil Company*, which is stated promises "to become one of the largest manufacturing and export concerns in Scotland". This was due to the very extensive minerals in the vicinity affording ample employment for several years before the wealth is expected to be exhausted. They added the boom in work new houses had been erected for the workers. This was likely the Clippens Rows, as the houses at Clippens Square were already extant.

Recognising the limitations of coal-oil production in Renfrewshire, the *Clippens Oil Company* acquired lease of oil shales at Midlothian in 1879 and began the development of the *Pentland Oil Works*. Crude oil production then ceased at Clippens, although the refinery remained active until 1890, processing much of the crude oil produced at Pentland.

Ordinance Survey maps do not record *Clippens Oil Works* in operation but, given the large volume of waste material around the site, it is probable that the *Clippens Oil Works* and refinery occupied this site that the *Sun Iron Foundry* (shown in the 1897 map) would occupy from 1894.

This presumption is backed-up by an article in the *Greenock Telegraph and Clyde Shipping Gazette* on the 13th of April 1895. In the section 'Chief Sanitary Inspector's Report' it was referenced that "The Clippens Oil Works Company has likewise transferred their premises to the Sun Foundry Co., and this work is giving employment to a large number of persons".

Ironstone and shale minerals from Clippens Pits No's 1 & 2 were sited here, as were the bings created from the excavated materials, making it an ideal location for the Clippens company to easily source shale for their oil extraction process, and later for the *Sun Iron Foundry* to source ironstone to smelt into iron to cast and forge their products.

During the operations of the oil extraction process, oil shale rock was extracted from shafts and mines (unless purchased elsewhere) and was then brought to the nearby oil works. In these works, the shale rock was heated in retorts at temperatures of around 500 degrees Celsius to extract crude oil vapour that could then be condensed and further refined into useful oil fractions (the waste blaes being removed after heating and this evaporation was complete). The major product of the industry was paraffin (kerosene) for lighting, but other products included ammonium sulphate used in fertilisers, heavy oil, machine and lubricating oils, sulphuric acid, and, later, petrol and detergents.

One of the by-products of this oil extraction process was shale ash, or blaes, which was utilised by the Clippens company for manufacturing bricks at their nearby Brickworks.

In 1873 it was reported that a serious accident had occurred the *Clippens Shale-Oil Works* when an arch-roof of a large brick kiln caved-in on top of five men sat at a breakfast table. They men all received serious injuries, although once attended to by doctors at the scene, one of them was taken to the Infirmary and the other four allowed to go home.

The *Dundee Evening Telegraph* reported that on the 16th of August 1877, a boy called Neil Leitch, residing Linwood, was killed at the Clippens Shale Oil Works. He had been emptying waggon of coals, fell off the waggon, and a piece of coal striking him on the chest inflicted injuries from which he died two hours later as he was being carried home on a stretcher. The boy's father was killed in a similar manner several years ago at Bridge of Weir.

The *North British Daily Mail* reported on the 03rd of April 1878, details of a serious fire at the *Clippens Shale Oil Works*, resulting in £10,000 of damages. The fire started at 3.30pm and spread rapidly. Mr Bailie Love of Johnstone, who happened to be at the work at the time on business, mounted hie horse and rode swiftly to Johnstone for the fire brigade, which it turned out and was at the scene of the fire in a remarkably short space of time. By the time of their arrival, however, the entire building was in a blaze, and the flames were ascending upwards of 150 feet into the air, this causing considerable alarm in all the districts around. The Johnstone Fire Brigade worked with a will, and utilised every drop of water available from the cooling tanks in the works. The fire lasted until 9pm the following night due to the great amount of stored oil product. The origin of the fire couldn't be ascertained, but it is supposed to have arisen from overheating. The Police were present with a large force and protected the works from the invasion of those curious to approach too near the fire. It was not expected that the fire would lead to any of the workers to be thrown out of employment, as their assistance would be all the more needed to rectify matters so that other portions of the work will not be at stand-still.

The *Paisley Daily Express* reported on the 17th of June 1889, that members (Students) of the *Glasgow and West of Scotland Technical College Chemical and Metallurgical Society*, visited the works. They were shown around the works in two groups by the Clippens company Chemists and saw the various stages of refining the crude oil and *"received a most interesting description from their respective leaders"*.

The *Glasgow Herald* reported on the 14th of September 1899, that the operations of the company had been stopped since the 14th of July 1897, and from that date, there had been no output of shale whatever from the mines. The result was that the retorts and refineries had been lying silent and unused for almost two years. The workmen had been dismissed and had left the neighbourhood. The cause of the stoppage of the mines was the interdict of the *Edinburgh and District Water Trust* brought against them for working across the whole of the field. The result of the stoppage was that the mines were in a state of collapse, and it would take at least two years to re-open the works.

The *Clippens Oil Company* decided to voluntarily wind up the business on the 05th of May 1908, went into liquidation on the 28th of May 1910 – selling-off their Land, property, buildings and machinery in the process, and finally wound up the business on the 03rd of January 1912.

Mining industry locations to the northwest side of Linwood - map circa 1933.

Bings

Linwood's several Bings were man-made piles of mining waste material discarded mainly during the late 19th Century. In the case of the oil extraction process, it is was said that for every gallon of oil produced, seven tons of waste blaes was generated.

The colours of the Bings scattered around the Linwood area depended spoil material they were made up of, i.e., rusty orange-brown colour signified iron contents (e.g., Brediland), whereas untreated coal-shale would be black (e.g., Fulton), and shale that had been heated to great temperatures in the oil extraction process, would be a light brown colour (e.g., Middleton).

Linwood kids loved playing on the bings in the 1960's and 1970's, before they were moved. They'd slide down the loose slopes on tarpaulin sheets, breadboards, and the like.

People may wonder what became of the bings, where were they moved to, and for which purpose. The material from them was often used in the construction industry as fill material, or more usually as base material for major roads such as motorways. In the case of the Fulton bing we know that the material was moved and used at the *Royal Ordinance Factory* in Bishopton, presumably as cover material for their underground munitions manufacturing facilities. All Linwood's bings had been removed by the end of the 1970's.

Bing ex-Clippens Pits 2 & 3, formed from waste shale blaes material from oil extraction process at nearby Clippens Oil Works. New houses at Kinnaird Drive shown – circa 1963.

Part of the Fulton Bing ex-Fulton Pits No's 1 & 2, formed from excavated black shale excavated. Was situated between Linwood High and East Fulton Schools – circa early 1970's.

Middleton Road traversing picture showing [from left to right] Moss [Toll House] Cottage, another small house, football park where Linwood

Thistle played, their pavilion, a house that would later be used as part of the Tomato Sheds business, The large Bing at the back is spoil from the local mines. None of this remains, except the Bowling Green to the right.

Brickworks

Brickwork manufacturing works sprung up in many areas in the late 19th Century when it was realised that bricks could be made using blaes, a waste product from the mining industry.

Workers revealed how labourers in these grimy factories resembled black slaves because they were encrusted from head to foot in dark stour. Noise from manufacturing machinery reverberated so loudly that employees could only communicate above the din with hand and finger signs. Intense heat from blazing kilns and furnaces caused workers to perspire sooty sweat.

The *Glasgow Herald* reported on the 08th of April 1898 of a new company called *The Linwood Brickmaking Company Limited*, which would carry on the business of brick and tile making, with £10,000 Capital divided into 10,000 shares of £1 each. These works were located about 100m south of the junction of todays' Pearson Place and Lochhead Avenue, just at the northern side of the Perimeter Road. This business seems to have lasted until 1917 as that's when an auction was advertised in a newspaper to in order to sell-off their Plant, Machinery and Buildings.

The *Clippens Brickworks* started business in 1873 . Its precise location cannot be confirmed, but it is thought it was adjacent to its Clippens No's 1 and 2 pits, where the east-side entrance is to today's ON-X Sports complex, just off Brediland Road. Also unknown is when their making of bricks ceased, but it is known that it lasted at least into the 1990's, and that owners the *Clippens Oil Company* wound up their business in 1908, and went into liquidation in 1910.

When the pits closed at the turn of the 19th/20th Centuries, brickworks opened up at Blackstoun, Inkerman and Walkinshaw, using the waste materials from the bings.

Blackstoun (aka Blackstone) Brickworks operated form 1871, probably until 1917 as that's when an auction was advertised in a newspaper to in order to sell-off their Plant, Machinery, Buildings, and Miscellaneous effects.

The *Inkerman Brickworks* began in 1895 and it continued working right up until the end of the 1950's, presumably because they still had a source of blaes to make their bricks, and long after the village had been demolished in 1940. The *Inkerman Brickworks* was demolished in 1960.

Walkinshaw Brickworks was three storeys tall and dominated by a smoky chimney stack, and a slate-roofed factory. The works continued making bricks until the 1960's. In 1986, owners *British Airport Authority* announced that they were to demolish the *Walkinshaw Brickworks* near their Glasgow Airport.

It was here that a calamitous event unfolded in February 1912, when a gang of workers were walking home one stormy night after a long day's shift. They'd turned off Greenock Road into Candren Road, near Paisley Racecourse, when they were struck by forked lightning. James McCrudden, 52, received the full impact on his head and chest. His cloth cap was shredded and he perished instantly. His colleagues survived unscathed but severely shocked. A police constable arrived but James lay by the roadside until a Doctor Gardner arrived from Paisley to confirm his death. It was feared witnesses would be electrocuted if they touched his frazzled body. James, who had a wife and eight children, lived at 156 Inkerman Rows.

Brediland Chemical Works

In 1939, Paisley firm *Brediland Chemical Works* took over some of the buildings left over by the *Sun Iron Foundry* at what is the junction between Erskinefauld Road and Green Farm Road, and probably the same buildings previously used by the Clippens Shale Oil Works. It is unclear what the nature of their business was, but possibly linked with abundance of mined mineral close by. However, it should be noted that they had already been in business in Paisley since the mid-19th Century making a form of liquid manure. It is also uncertain when they closed their business, but they were certainly in this location throughout the 1940's and at least the early part of the 1950's, and the *Ordinance Survey* map from 1957 shows the buildings as *disused*. New houses, roads, and streets were built in its place from 1962.

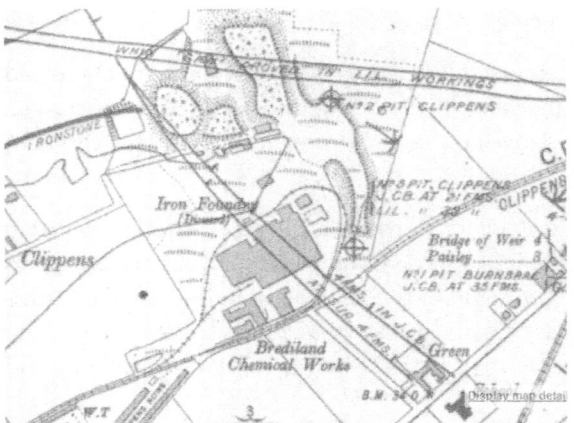

Mining map – circa early-1900's. Future (1939) Brediland Chemical Works buildings to South and disused main Foundry building to the North. Railway circulating both works. Long bing to North-East. Green Farm Road to South.

Aerial photo looking from North to South – circa 1940. Smoke coming out of Brediland Chemical Works Chimney. Sun Iron Foundry now gone. Rail tracks still visible and long bing at foot of photo. Green Farm Road top-left of photo

The Sun Foundry Ltd

The firm was founded by George Smith at 64 Port Dundas Road, Glasgow in 1858. They advertised themselves as *Art Metal Workers, Iron Founders and Sanitary Engineers*, and *Artistic Iron Founders*, and displayed their wares at their show yard in Bothwell Street in Glasgow.

The firm later relocated to Parliamentary Road in Glasgow, and later opened a foundry in 1994 at Clippens, near Linwood. The foundry was situated where Oxford Drive and Kilbrennan Road are located today. From the iron ore mined there the cast what today they call 'Street Furniture'. Amongst the Sun Foundry's finest (although not made in Linwood) and most elaborate public works is the huge ornamental Fountain in Fountain Gardens, Paisley, complete with walruses, cherubs and crocodiles, which was commissioned by the Paisley thread manufacturer Thomas Coats in 1868.

The *Glasgow Herald* reported on the 24th of May 1894 on the *"The formal inauguration of the new Sun Foundry Works"* as follows. *"...Linwood folks are happy over the fact of this industrial hive locating itself into their neighbourhood. Already rents have stiffened considerably, and houses of the better class could he let readily if enterprising builders saw their way to erect such within easy distance of the works. The company's houses at present forms a small village called Clippens. Everything about Clippens (the new sphere of operations) has undergone or is undergoing change and re-construction. Within three months new buildings covering thousands of square feet (one of in them alone covers 70,000 square feet) have sprung up, immense areas of undulating surface have been levelled and floored, ponderous and intricate machinery of the latest types have been erected, uninviting sheets of grimy, oleaginous water, formerly so conspicuous at Clippens, have passed out of sight, and in their stead stable terra-firma carrying railways in all directions re over the works have been created. Such work has been accomplished here within nine weeks speaks volumes alike for the enterprise of the firm and for the push of the contractor. The firm has for some time been principally for artistic castings, and has been fortunate to win many orders from French and Italian competitors. They are at present modelling some large fountains, all for abroad, and have several structures, immense ones, in hands for foreign*

Governments. It may be added that the works and houses cover an area of 463 acres, and every appliance for the efficient and economical production of their manufactures has been adopted."

Then, just less than three years later, the *Paisley & Renfrewshire Gazette* reported on the 27th of February 1897, that *"Messrs. Hodge A Smith. C.A., Glasgow, agents for the Sun Foundry. Limited, have issued the following circular: —"We beg to inform you that Messrs. George Smith & Co., Sun Foundry (Limited), Clippens, by Linwood, Renfrewshire, registered office of the company 26 Robertson Street, Glasgow, having resolved on winding up the affairs of the company under voluntary liquidation, have appointed our Mr. James Robert Hodge as liquidator. The resolution to wind up the company has been brought matters extraneous to their commercial trailing. While as little delay possible will take place in realising the assets, we think right to add that there is no expectation of the assets being sufficient to pay the debts of the company."*

The creation of a foundry in 1994 in Linwood suggests that the company was starting to struggle. It is somewhat curious that Sun Foundry did not appear to embrace the constructional opportunities of cast iron for building which its rival Saracen and Lion foundries did with much success.

It was a gradual winding-up and the foundry finally closed its doors in 1899.

Land Contamination Legacy of the Mining Related and other Heavy Industries

Oil from Shale Extraction Process

A solid waste material called semi-coke is the main by-product of oil shale pyrolysis, which is produced in large quantities and causes severe environmental pollution. Waste material from the shale oil industry also consisted of several pollutants including sulphates, heavy metals, and polycyclic aromatic hydrocarbons (PAHs), some of which are toxic and carcinogenic. To avoid contamination of the groundwater, the solid waste from the thermal treatment process was disposed in open dumps such as bings or landfill, not underground where it could potentially reach clean ground water.

Since 2007 there have been reports of a Tar-like substance oozing from the ground near the *ON-X Sports Centre*, Running Track, and *Woodlands Community Bowling Club*.

In 2010, *Renfrewshire Council* began an exhaustive investigation to find out if there was pollution under the ground, after small amounts of black tar started coming to the surface in the Erskinefauld area. *"The council has thoroughly checked the ground their homes stand on and they can be rest assured it is safe. We have consulted closely with NHS Greater Glasgow and Clyde and expert advisers on the results of the investigation. They have confirmed that there is no need for a major clean-up on health grounds. Our investigation also involved a wide-ranging review of health statistics. This showed there is no difference between the health of people in Linwood and anywhere else in the west of Scotland."*

Positive results gave the all-clear for new houses to be built *Machrie Crescent*, which were completed in 2014. However, this sampling and testing was on the land of the former grassy park land area between Brediland and Erskinefauld Roads, but it is not clear if any sampling and testing has been done for the land around the current *Woodlands Community Bowling Club, Linstone Sheltered Housing*, skateboard park, golf course area, and running track.

The Clippens Shale Oil Company Ltd was sited nearby [junction of Erkinefauld and Green Farm Roads] and produced crude oil and refining products during period from 1870 to 1890. And these buildings were taken over in 1939 by the *Brediland Chemical Works*. It's questionable how waste was discarded. Some speculate in 'tar-pits' scattered around the area. If so, then we shouldn't be surprised when we see Tar-like substance oozing from the ground still. Because of this, it seems to me that this land was never treated properly and may still pose a toxic and carcinogenic danger to the public. All these homes and sports facilities have been built on top of contaminated land, with no attempt made to treat the land beforehand. The blame for this is I suspect, is either wholly, or at least mostly, with the *Clippens Shale Oil Company Ltd*, who had two mines, a Brickworks and Chemical works in the area for several decades.

East Fulton Shale Oil Works was listed in *Watson's Paisley Directory* as being owned by *James Liddell & Co., Crude Oil Makers, East Fulton Oil Works* (1874-78), although the works were constructed in 1868 and likely dismantled in 1885. The location is uncertain, but was likely to be associated with a waste bing directly south of East Fulton farm, and marked on the 1897 Ordinance Survey map. The bing was removed in the 1970's, but it is questionable as to why the land between East Fulton and Linwood High Schools has never been built upon. If it were only shale waste in the bing, then there would be little contamination in the ground, if any. It may be that the land there is contaminated with hazardous wastes from the oil from shale extraction process.

A similar point is made about the *Inkerman Oil Works*, which has been known at various times as *Abercorn Oil Works, Walkinshaw Oil Works and Hermand Oil Works*. This area of land, which also had an Ironstone pit, a bing, a clay pit and the *Walkinshaw Brickworks*, was used as landfill in the 1970's and 1980's, then grassed over with methane emission pipes evident and being monitored.

Other Processes

Regarding the *Brediland Chemical Works*, which operated from 1939 to early 1950's, it is not clear what their business was, and any waste that may have come from it, but it may not have been related to oil extraction from shale. An 1870 newspaper advert of their operation in the Brediland area of Paisley, shows that their business then was in the production of agricultural products.

Any contaminants from waste products at *Sun Iron Foundry* smelting process would be minimal and would certainly not create a tar-like substance. Likewise, any contaminants emanating from the kilns of the *'The Linwood Brickmaking Company Limited'* and the *'The Clippens Brickworks Company'*, would be minimal.

Semi-Coke, the biggest by-product and waste material emanating from the process of extracting oil from shale. It was toxic and was usually stored in form of large bings.

The Sun Foundry with todays' overlaying map. Two buildings at foot are the Brediland Chemical Works. Top is Clippens Oil Works, middle if Clippens Brick Works.

The Linwood Foundry Company

The Linwood Foundry was operating in Linwood, at the west end of Bridge Street, in the first half of the 20th Century. The firm regularly advertised for people to send them old "2nd hand horizontal Diesel Engines", "Diesel and Paraffin Engines" and "Side-Tipping Wagons", for which they asked "what price is required". What they done with these items, I'm not sure, but perhaps with their facilities they could refurbish them, then sell them on.

Paper Mill

The North British Daily Mail reported on the 21st of April 1874 "Linwood – New Factory. Mr Watson, Linwood, has arranged for the opening of a new paper manufactory in the village, which will employ a number of hands. Cotton spinning, which has for many years been the staple trade of the district is at present in a very depressed condition".

R. & W. Watson Ltd had been established by two brothers, Robert and William, originally apprenticed to a Derbyshire paper mill, had moved up to Scotland to start their own business due to their attraction to the supply of water and readily available supply of local labour.

The firm originally moved into the old Henderson's part of the Cotton Mill, and through the next two decades up to 1994 they slowly took over all of the former Cotton Mill when that industry finally ceased in Linwood for good a few months before. During this period, they had made great improvements and modifications to suit their scope of business.

By 1903 the firm had '160 hands', and by the 1950s the firm was flourishing and employed almost 500 workers. They specialised in the manufacture of tissue paper manilla envelopes and sealings, as well as UK Car License documents. As the firm developed it moved into strong papers for cable insulation in the electrical industry and gun cartridge paper for munitions requirements. They even made the extremely strong paper for the ejector seats of aircraft. The firm exported all over the world although its main market was within the UK.

A tragedy occurred on the at approximately 3.45pm on the 07th of October 1968 when, as a fire took hold of the Paper Mill buildings, which had been reported to the Johnstone Fire Station an hour earlier, the west wall collapsed and trapped four crew members. Rescue operations were mounted and three members of the fire crew were recovered alive, but sadly the fourth member, Edmund Burt, had been killed by the falling masonry. The building was so severely damaged and in such a dangerous condition that arrangements were made to have it demolished immediately and the work of demolition started that same evening.

By 1974 Scottish paper makers, *Tullis Russell*, has bought R. & W. Watson (Converters), and their marketing company, *Grange Fibre*. This move is seen as a natural extension for Tullis Russell as they took over supply of the Linson Products base paper in 1972 when Watson discontinued paper making at Linwood. The move was welcomed by Watson, both as a means of strengthening their financial base, and as security for their future paper supplies.

By the early 1980's they had become *Watson Grange paper convertors*, who mainly provided coatings for books. They were by now an employee-owned company, but still under the Tullis Russell group.

In 1984 the factory was evacuated due to a disgruntled worker making a hoax phone-call to the factory's office to say that there was a bomb about to go off. 50 workers evacuated the building quickly. It was reported in the local newspaper covering the trial, that he done this because he didn't like doing the backshift.

Watson Grange paper convertors continued into the early 2000's and closed. The paper industry in Linwood was also dead now.

R & W Watson Ltd Paper Mill in centre of photo, circa 1933.

The Paper end product coming off the rollers at the Paper Mill.

Linwood lady Sarahanne Doyle kindly provided me with copies of hand written notes left by her dear Papa John McSporran (1927-2017). In it he recounts his education and move into employment in the Paper Mill.

"Started in Linwood Public [aka Wee Red] School in February 1932 and remained there until February 1939, learning Arithmetic, English, early History, and Geography. I was good at History and Geography, not so good at English, [although] not bad at spelling.

Went to Camphill Secondary School in Paisley, February 1939 and was a pupil there until January 1941. Left school at the end of January 1941 aged 14 years of age.

Started in R & W Watson Paper Mill on Tuesday 4th of February 1941. They owned the two tenements where I lived, Armour Place and Bridge Street. On leaving the house I walked 30 yards to the Mill Gatehouse entrance and sent to work in the Laboratory earning 10 shillings a week for 6 days a week including Saturday mornings 8am to 12pm noon.

In 1941, 10 shillings was equivalent of 50 pence in 2010"

John worked up his way up at the R & W Watson Paper Mill to the position of Senior Quality Controller and worked there all his days until retiring in 1992 at age 65."

Perhaps circa 1970's: John McSporran working away at his job as a Senior Quality Controller at R & W Watson Paper Mill.

Power Generating Plant – Linwood Paper Mill

1933: Armour Place tenement - on Bridge Street, erected in 1897. The Paper Mill and Napier Street shown in the background.

2023 Bridge Street: The Armour Place tenement would have been approx. here, from where John McSporran would have walked the 30 yards to the Mill Gatehouse.

ENGINEERING

Reid Gear Co Ltd

Reid Gear Co Ltd, Napier Street, Linwood, Renfrewshire was set up in 1897 in the old Picking Hall of Henderson's Cotton Mill, the Managing Director being Mr Thomas Reid, and he in turn was to be followed by a further four Thomas Reid's in the firm long history.

In 1907 the *Reid Gear Company* reported a trade boom. It had enjoyed wonderful success since its inception ten years before and just had just completed a feu contract to include seven acres of ground suitable for the extension of their works. This news proved most gratifying to the inhabitants of the village, who naturally expected greet prosperity to follow. Several other smaller businesses in the village were also very busy at this time, and making preparations for extensions. The result was that a number of new houses were being erected and Linwood sprung into a bustle of energy the like of which it had never known before.

The site at the north end of Napier Street, consisted of a range of late, 19th Century buildings containing a quantity of machinery. The main engineering workshop was a 7-bay, north-lit, brick-built structure, with a pattern makers' wood workshop and an asbestos cement-clad building where the larger gears were cut (winch test tower), together with administrative and engineers' offices.

Reid's specialised in manufacturing marine instruments, deck machinery for ships and gears for a wide spread of manufacturing industry. They also provided traction gearing for the high-speed Intercity train and *London Underground* has been a major customer.

In the last thirty years or so of its existence, *Reid Gear* were subject to a significant down turn in engineering and shipbuilding in the West of Scotland and Western Europe. Its customer base has been rapidly declining as the shipbuilding industry has virtually disappeared in the UK, and this unfortunately sealed the deal. The works closed in 2008 with around 50 skilled engineers being made unemployed.

The Reid Gear Coompany - 1897-2008

Dent and Co and Johnson – 1912-16.

Dent and Co and Johnson

Dent and Co and Johnson set up in Linwood at the corner of Bridge of Weir Road and Duke Street [now a continuation of Fulwood Avenue] in 1912. They were engineers and makers of scientific and navigational instruments, clocks, press tools, compasses, and record player until they closed in 1960. The building they used was demolished in 1966 as it was considered radioactive from the making of luminous dials for military and civilian use. The rubble and soil were taken away for safe disposal, but the cleared land remains unoccupied today as it's still considered to be contaminated by radium; a radioactive element used to illuminate the dials of scientific devices they made. The land is still is regularly tested for radioactivity. An unconfirmed account from a former employee some years ago was that *"many women who worked at the factory developed mouth cancer from licking to moisten brushes used in the illuminating process"*.

Crossroads of Bridge of Weir Road, Bridge Street, Duke Street (later Fulwood Ave), and Moss Road – circa 1964. Two men are sitting on a bench at what was also known as 'Dent's Corner'. The Dent and Co and Johnson factory dominates the picture on the left, and at top right is the land being developed for the Golden Pheasant Hotel and Car Park.

The Eclipse Tool Co., Ltd

The Eclipse Tool Co., Ltd., was registered with the limited liability companies during the week commencing 19th of March 1906, with a capital of £5000, in 5000 shares of each, to acquire and continue the business of the company of this name, now in liquidation, and to trade as mechanical and electrical engineers, toolmakers, contractors, makers of machines, engines, appliances, and magnetic and electric apparatus. Shareholders included Wm. John Hart Reid, engineer, and members of the Galbraith's grocery chain. It operated out of a factory in Napier Street.

The Farnham and Whyte Machine Company

Little is known about this company, but we can form an idea from its apparent bankruptcy sale on 14th Feb 1923, as a whole at starting price of £8,667.00. Plant and Machinery (very little used), Rackham Engine Patent Rights, Jigs, Tools, Electrical Installations, Fixture and Fittings, and Furniture. Existing Contracts for Lighting Power and Telephone. The buildings consisted of a Machine Shop, Gate House, Office, Dwelling House, as well as an annex consisting of Smithy and a Drawing Office.

It would seem to have been an engineering firm that manufactured and possibly installed lighting and telecommunications products.

Tod and Dickson

Tod and Dickson's (T&D) original Joinery workshop was at the right-hand side of the entrance to the Public Park behind Lee Place - at least from the early 1930's. It was 'Incorporated' in 1961 when it moved to Stirling Drive, at what would be the junction with Gilmartin Road when it was built later that decade. This old building all that remained in Linwood of the mining industry and had been the Engine House for the old adjacent Fulton Blackband and Blueband Ironstone Mine No. 1, from which the 'waste' shale was dumped to form the adjacent shale bing. T&D was 'Struck-off' in 1992 and the old building demolished in 1995. However, the T&D Company Number: SC136426 was 'Restored' at Companies House on the 13th of September 2019, and then later 'Dissolved' on the 04th of April 2023.

William Beardmore & Company's

The *William Beardmore* complex on the north side of the Linwood Road originally developed in the late 1930s, as part of the shadow war factory programme, for the manufacture of special steels and gun barrels, armaments, aeroplane components and even tanks. The plant not only built tanks, but repaired and refurbished damaged machines sent back from the front. Armament worker, blonde haired 18-year-old Paisley girl Elizabeth Sellars was picked to sit atop the first tank produced at this plant when it was rolled-out during the war years.

In 1942 the plant was also earmarked to cover the munitions work and gunworks done in Sheffield in case it was damaged by bombing.

It was managed by the Glasgow engineering company, *William Beardmore* who later used the facility for manufacturing railway rolling stock, wheels , axles wagons and other items such as steel ingots.

William Beardmore & Company Ltd Linwood Factory – circa 1942. Elizabeth Sellars as model to sit atop the first tank produced.

William Beardmore & Company Ltd – circa 1940's. LLinwood Factory on north side of Linwood Road.

Pressed Steel Company Ltd

In 1947, an Oxford firm, the *Pressed Steel Company Ltd.*, producers of all-steel motor-car bodies, took over a large part of the Government factory at Linwood Road, Paisley, for an extension of their manufacturing capacity. In an announcement from the *Scottish Regional Office of the Board of Trade* it is stated that the factory has been transferred from the *Ministry of Supply to the Board of Trade* and would be managed by *Scottish Industrial Estates Ltd*. Part of the factory would be operated as before for ingot steel production by *William Beardmore & Co., Ltd*, as agents for the *Ministry of Supply*. By the end of the year the level of output was expected to reach 2500 tons a week. The buildings at Linwood Road were already being adapted and the necessary production equipment had either been ordered or would be transferred from the *Pressed Steel Company's* works at Cowley, near Oxford. It was expected that some manufacturing activities would begin at Linwood Road before the end of that year.

The Government of the day was anxious to combat the problem of high unemployment in the area, and offered *Pressed Steel* generous terms to move to Linwood. It also appears to have placed few conditions over what was manufactured at the plant. *Pressed Steel* initially manufactured railway rolling stock, railway wagons, farm machines, and refrigeration equipment, but, with a decline in orders, transferred much of its production to body panels for *Ford* and *BMC* lorry cabs.

By 1950 the labour force was just over 300, but within a year had increased to 1100, and 100 16-ton all-steel mineral wagons were being turned out weekly for *British Railways*. This meant that a wagon came off the assembly line every 26 minutes.

The *Pressed Steel* built the 'Blue Trains' from 1959, which served the north bank of Clydebank. In the same year they fabricated the bodies 100 Swedish *Volvo* Sports P.1800 model cars per week with a workforce of 2000 and rising.

The following year in 1960 they also made the bodies of *Rover Luxury Saloon* car with 3000 workers employed, and several hundred planned to be taken on.

By 1963 *Pressed Steel* had an alliance with *Chrysler UK* in making bodies for the new Hillman Imp model. However, it had reached its capacity in production and now employed 5800.

In 1964 they received an injection of capital from *Chrysler UK*, with 30 per cent of *Rootes'* shares going to the US company; by 1969 they had come under full Chrysler ownership.

In 1967, the Linwood Pressed Steel factory was bought by *Rootes Chrysler*, following *BMC's* acquisition of *Pressed Steel's* Cowley and Swindon sites.

Blackstoun Engineering Works / Rubery Owen

The *Blackstoun Engineering Works* factory initially made window frames in a large fabrication and assembly shop situated in area locally known as 'horses park', and where back end of Greenhill Drive would later be built in 1975. Its products were sold through a shop outlet at 145 Bath Street, Glasgow, called *McLean & Co*. Known as 'Blackburn's' by locals, the company was in business between the early 1930's and 1939 when it was commandeered for the War effort.

The factory then switched to the manufacture of parts for *Sunderland flying boats* for the Government up until early 1945, which was several months before WWII ended.

On the 24th of January 1945, the *Minister of Supply* announced in the *House of Commons* that the factory would now, turn out Cupboard Units for Prefabricated Houses, and that this would help with the housing problem in Scotland. He further stated that this information came to him from a high official of the *Rubery Owen company of Darlaston*, South Staffs, who would be taking over the war-time factory by the spring for the production of household fitments. The factory would later return to making metal-framed windows and caravan frames and chassis as well. The factory closed in the early 1970's, was demolished, and made way for the new Greenhill Drive/Crescent estate completed in 1975.

Sawmill

The Sawmill was founded *by James Kennedy & Co., Ltd* in 1951 on the site of the old Balaclava hamlet from the mid-19th century, which within a few years became Clippens Square and Clippens Rows before they were demolished in the 1940's. The works continued there until around 1970 when they were in turn demolished to make way for St Andrews Primary School soon afterwards.

The Blackstoun Works in indicated in this advert from 1934.   Linwood Sawmill from the air – circa 1963.

Dairies

It seems that there was a dairy business at 26 Napier Street at the turn of the 19th and 20th Centuries. This is indicated in an advert in the *Paisley & Renfrewshire Gazette* on the 31st of March 1900, whereby is describes a *"Dairy premises to-let consisting of Byre, Outhouses, Shop and Dwelling-House of Two Rooms and a Kitchen – presently occupied by Mr John Prentice."*

The Renfrew family, headed by Andrew, ran a dairy out of 31 Napier Street in the second half of the 20th Century. They supplied homes and businesses in Paisley, Renfrew, Linwood and Barrhead. As the business expanded Mr Andrew Renfrew managed to purchase the vacant St. Conval's school site next door and convert into a dairy and built a new house for himself. Over the years the business employed hundreds of milk boys from Linwood village and I still bump into some of them in my travels, many happy memories from these days. Today members of the Renfrew family still reside in houses around the original site of the dairy.

Car Plant

As the existence of Linwood village owes itself to the creation of the Cotton Mill in 1792, the existence of the new and vastly expanded Linwood town owes itself to the creation of the *Rootes* Car Plant, and all the opportunities that brought with it. Thousands of workers, the bulk of them coming from Glasgow, poured into Linwood with the guarantee of a job and a 'back and front door' house with it for their young families, but of course many were housed in maisonette flats also.

The Rootes Group had selected the 'Linwood' site for a number of reasons. The first of these reasons was that it was within the Government determined "distressed area" zone, and certain financial backing was available. The second reason was that it was close to the *Pressed Steel* factory, which was already turning out a variety of car bodies. It is not clear why the location was deemed 'Linwood', as the Rootes factory, the *William Beardmore & Company*, and the *Pressed Steel Co. Ltd*, were never within Linwood's borders, but were half in Paisley, and half in Elderslie, either side of Linwood Road. It was perhaps because Linwood was the place where the bulk of the development would be made in terms of housing and regional shopping centre.

Rootes Motors Ltd opened their new car factory close to Linwood in 1963, and next to the *Pressed Steel* factory which it later bought over. The first model made in the factory was the Hillman Imp. In 1967 the *Chrysler Corporation* took over, and continued production with the Hillman Hunter and the Hillman Avenger. However, the factory was troubled by low sales and high production costs, and a series of industrial disputes. In 1975 the government stepped in with financial aid in a bid to prevent job losses, and a new car - the Chrysler Sunbeam - was launched. The company's troubles continued. In 1979 the French car firm *Peugeot-Citroen* took over, and renamed the company *Talbot*, but still the company lost money. In May 1981 the car plant closed, making thousands of people unemployed. This was a severe blow to the economy of Linwood and the surrounding areas.

Reasons for the Failure of the Car Plant

In their article on the 26th of October 1972, the *Aberdeen Press and Journal* reported on the remarks of the managing director of *Chrysler (UK)* Mr Gilbert Hunt, who was speaking before a Commons committee of M.P.'s inquiring into incentives for regional development memorandum on Linwood produced for M.P.s by the company. He was quoted as saying that if his company had not opened a plant at Linwood, Renfrewshire, "*our cars would be cheaper and we would sell more.*" He went on to say that "*they had gone Linwood to fulfil a social obligation*", and that "*were there no industrial development certificates or constraint, we would undoubtedly have developed in Coventry as we had plenty of spare room there*". So, it seems that *Chrysler* regretted ever coming to Linwood and taking over the car plant from *Rootes*, in the first place.

The reasons why the car plant didn't prosper and eventually died, are complex and numerous. This subject would require a whole book on its own. Here I give a brief overview of possible reasons and how it seemed to me as a person growing up in Linwood, and whose father had worked in the car plant for a few years.

The American owners *Rootes* brought in their modern ways of management, which weren't understood or liked by the workforce.

In her 2010 PhD Thesis *'Examining the 'hard-boiled bunch': work culture and industrial relations at the Linwood car plant, c. 1963-1981'*, Linwood's Alison Julia Gilmour points out issues from both workers and management that would cause the clashes that lead to workers discontent and walk-outs:

"A process of de-industrialisation saw workers from the heavy industries, such as ship-building, seek employment at Linwood, and the resulting failure to adjust to the different nature of work accompanied the transference of workplace militancy from the traditional sector to new industries therefore, contributing to poor industrial relations" One worker interviewed stated:

"Ah know that a huge amount of the personnel that came to Linwood to work in the plant were from the shipyards, an ah've read on Linwood the books and so on and it confirms a lot. It really just puts into place what a saw as a boy that, all the shipyard practices came and because of that you had the union attitudes, the one man, one job, you had the management were not to be trusted, the management are a bunch of bastards, the management are this and the management are that".

Bill Reid, who had direct experience of working in the personnel department at the Linwood plant, was interviewed and commented on his experience within the industrial relations:

"Ah think one was as bad as the other. Ah say my experience in the, the personnel side, if they saw a way to mess somebody around, they did it, and eh ah was amazed. Ah'm not sayin it happened all the time, but I caught, caught on a couple of occasions, "Oh him, aye right we'll do that", and ah thought no wonder there's problems."

There was a disproportionate number of unofficial strikes occurred at Linwood and contributed to poor industrial relations. Indeed, within the Scottish car industry alone there were over three hundred strikes between 1963 and 1969. Such strikes tended to be directly related to events on the shop floor; seemingly an instantaneous response by the workforce. The prevailing dominant narrative tends to attribute the 'failure' of Linwood to difficult industrial relations arising from a clash between work cultures: craft-based bespoke production, an embedded feature of Scottish industrial work experience, and automated assembly.

Workforce peaks of 9,000 were reached in 1965, 1970 and 1974, followed in each case by damaging redundancy: 1,000 in September–October 1966, another 1,000 by increments in 1971, and more than 2,000 late in 1974.

Workers Excuses for Downing Tools and Walking Out

There are many excuses as to why the workforce walked out and went home from work, too many examples to mention. Some of them have a semblance of justifiable reason, but others just seem too militant and incredibly ridiculous. Below I have listed a few examples; make your own mind up.

The *Liverpool Echo* reported on the 03rd of March 1966 under the headline *"Car Plants Shut"* where it explains that *"The Rootes Hillman Imp and Singer Chamois factories at Linwood, Renfrewshire, were shut down to-day and the 2,000 workers sent home. Car production was brought to a standstill by an electrical fault which could not be repaired because the factory's 22 maintenance electricians are already on strike."*

The *Birmingham Daily Post* reported on the 08th of December 1965 under the headline *"Football on TV stops Scottish car factories"*. The article tells that *"the live televising of the Scotland v. Italy World Cup football tie in Naples into Scottish homes yesterday brought production of the Rootes Hillman Imp car at Linwood, Renfrewshire, to a standstill. Almost 4,000 workers had to be sent home from the Rootes plant and the adjacent Pressed Steel Company factory where the car bodies are made because absenteeism was so high after lunch it was impossible to continue production. Scotland lost 3-0 and are now out of the World Cup."*

The *Liverpool Echo* reported on the 26th of May 1970 under the headline *"500 Strike"* and told that *"more than 500 men were on strike at the Rootes car plant, Linwood, Renfrewshire, today over the dismissal of a workmate. A further 250 had to be sent home."*

The *Coventry Evening Telegraph* reported on the 16th of June 1970 under the headline *"4,000 in Linwood Walkout"*. Apparently, *"About 4,000 workers walked out on strike today at the Rootes car factory at Linwood, Renfrewshire. The men held mass meetings to protest about a system of transfers to other Jobs. They claim that certain Jobs in the factory are better than others and hold that more of them should be given to men who have worked there for a considerable time. Too many they claim, have been given to newcomers."*

The *Coventry Evening Telegraph* reported on the 24th of August 1977 under the headline *"Strikers Return at Linwood"* where we were told that *"Chrysler's plant in Linwood was back in production today after strikers agreed to go back to work following union-management talks. This said both sides had agreed on a return-to-work starting with last night's shift, but there was no mention of the man at the centre of the row, a trim shop worker sacked on Monday after allegedly reporting drunk for work on Friday. Two hundred colleagues had earlier walked out on protest strike, bringing production at the plant where the new Sunbeam was launched two weeks ago to a standstill, with 2,000 of the 7,500 men idle."*

As you can see there was great variety of excuses to stop work. Workers would not only turn up for work drunk, but consume alcohol they had smuggled in whilst on duty. And there were sackings and subsequent walk-outs due to workers relieving themselves up against factory walls, instead of in the toilets. Linwood folklore even has it that there was a case whereby that *"because someone had cheese in their pieces, yet again, the men would down tools and walk out in sympathy."*

You may ask yourself, why it was that other car plants in the UK managed to be successful, and Linwood wasn't. Perhaps because the Linwood plant workers, many coming from the likes of Red Clydeside, were just more militant by nature. It seems that they didn't help themselves and often pushed the various owners of the car plant to far.

Things would come to a head with the *Conservative Party* winning the 1979 General Election; the writing was on the wall for the Linwood plant, as the Tories were about to destroy and wipe-out traditional industries throughout the UK during the 1980's.

The Hillman Imp was made by the Rootes Group and its successor Chrysler Europe from 1963 until 1976. Launched on 3rd of May 1963.

Imagined Menu for a 'Grand Chrysler Redundancy Dance', shows dissatisfaction with AEEU Engineering Union leader John Carty and Chrysler Corp. CEO John Ricarrdo.

Linwood Incinerator

The Linwood Incinerator was opened by Opened by HM Queen Elizabeth II in 1974. The opening ceremony was attended by many from Linwood, with all schools represented. The plant would continue until 1992 when it closed and was soon afterwards demolished. Throughout its life it was the subject of controversy in relation to damage to the environment and to the town people's health. Some of the concerns of the public are laid-out below.

Unknown waste from Holy Loch submarine base was regularly taken to the Linwood Incinerator during its period in operation and workers were instructed not to touch any of the Holy Loch waste by hand.

It is questionable if the Linwood Moss site should ever have been used as a landfill site, as by nature as a peat bog, and the fluids emanating from the landfill known as leachates, the effects of which can still be seen today all over the area.

SEPA could not offer any explanation as to why no records were available for Linwood Incinerator operations and nearby Linwood Moss landfill site prior to 1996. They said in 2007 *"The incinerator mentioned was closed in 1992 and again we have no records of which we are aware regarding how it was operated and whether wastes were partially burned or not."*

Linwood Incinerator on Middleton Road – circa 1974. Opened by HM Queen Elizabeth II in 1974, closed in 1992.

HM Queen Elizabeth II opens Linwood Incinerator on Wednesday the 03rd of July 1974.

Infrastructure, Services and Amenities

Linwood Cross – circa 1930's. Napier Street – from North [bottom] to South [top], being traversed by Bridge Street – Left to Right. Linwood Parish Church shown with Goods Station at rear, Lee Place is tenement building to the left and the Bucks Head Inn shown on corner of Linwood Cross. Allardyce's Garage between the two of them.

Post Service

On the 17th of December 1856, the *Glasgow Chronicle* reported that the *Post Office* had just began a new arrangement for the delivery and collection of letters to many residents in the towns and suburbs. The letters shall be delivered free, by runners, or 'letter-carriers', to the villages of Linwood, Balaclava, and Inkerman. All the dwelling houses and farms included within the district, will in future have their letters delivered free of charge, beyond the usual rates of postage. To all, and particularly to the mining population which had recently settled down in the now populous districts in the west, this will be of great importance. Over and above the expense which they will thus be relieved of, they will have secured to them a regular and punctual delivery. In the village itself the inhabitants are also to have a share in the additional means given to the public for communicating with each other by the erection of a pillar letter-box for the collection of letters.

Throughout the 19th and early 20th centuries, Linwood's main post office and telegraph office were located at No's 16 and 25 Napier Street respectively before they moved around the corner to Bridge Street next to the Park Place tenement. Then in early 1960's, the post office [incorporating telegrams] moved to temporary cabin in south Napier Street for about 6 years, then on to the to the new shopping centre just off Ardlamont Square in 1971. There is stayed until it was demolished in 2010 and returned in 2014 when *Tesco* shopping centre opened. There was a second post office at the Clippens shops from 1965 until around 2010 when the Newsagents shop it was housed in closed.

As reported in the *Paisley & Renfrewshire Gazette* on the 30th of September 1899, "The Government has, on the recommendation of Mr McMaster, Postmaster, supplied the Paisley Post Office with bicycle for the postman, on the Linwood District for the purpose of accelerating the delivery and to extend to other places."

Garage & Petrol Stations

From the early to mid-20th century there were two mechanics garages on Bridge Street which also sold petrol and diesel. These were Allardyce's and Donaldson's, the former across the other side of Bridge Street from entrance to Paper Mill, the later across from Craigends Masonic Lodge. Allerdyce's garage was demolished in early 1960's and the building is still in existence, but now with a different use. The Perimeter Garage and Petrol Station on the Perimeter Road was extant from 1971 right up to 2014 when the new *Tesco* petrol station was built on that spot after the former building was demolished.

Water Supply

Before the piped water supply was in-place, Linwood relied on several communal water taps for their drinking, washing and cooking needs. Known taps of that time are those listed here:

- One at the west side of where the Gospel Hall would later be
- Three at Clippens Square / Rows
- Three at Redan Rows
- Bridge and Napier Streets most likely had water taps too

However, it seems that the quality and safety of the drinking water was somewhat unreliable. The *Glasgow Weekly Mail* reported on the 09th of February 1867 that, *"the Parochial Board of Kilbarchan have received an analysis of for samples of water by Professor Penny, showing that two wells in the village Linwood are all more or less charged will noxious ingredients in the solution with the water, which could not be removed by any process of filtration, and recommending discontinuance of the water of one of the wells in Linwood. The committee agreed to the recommendation of the report."*

Linwood village first acquired piped running cold water from *Paisley Waterworks*, originating from the Braes of Gleniffer, when on the 01st of June 1872, the supply was turned on, at a cost of £622.

And Glasgow Herald had earlier reported on the 23rd of April 1872 that *"The Paisley Water Commissioners have agreed with the Clippens Shale Oil Company to continue their pipes from Linwood to their shale works, and to a village for the accommodation of the workers which is to be erected on adjacent ground"*.

The *Paisley & Renfrewshire Gazette* reported on the 02nd of 1897, that at a public meeting the previous Wednesday, and in commemoration of Queen Victoria's Diamond Jubilee celebrating her 60th anniversary of her accession, that Linwood should erect a 'small drinking fountain and horse trough'. However, it was decided to *"hold the matter over"* due to insufficient funds in the 'Diamond Jubilee Fund'.

The same newspaper reported on the 26th of April 1902, that a *"fountain be erected at the [Linwood] Cross"*, but again there was insufficient funds in the 'Linwood Jubilee Fund'.

There were also public drinking water fountains at the entrance to the Public Park from around 1930, and in the schools in Napier Streets in the late 19th and early 20th Centuries.

And it seems that it was the case that on some occasions there was difficulty in paying bills. On the 14th of April 1900, the newspaper reported that *"the water had been shut off from a Roman Catholic School"* [in Napier Street] for not paying the water rates. The Master of Works then reported that the water supply *"had since been turned on again, but future declinature to pay would result again in the water being turned off."*

Gas Supply

At a monthly meeting of *Renfrew County Council* on the 12th of July 1905, it was agreed to supply gas to Linwood at a cost of £200 for the sequestration of the piping and to supply the commodity to the inhabitants.

Mr Lauder was the Lamplighter, or *Leerie*, for several years in the village from around the 1940's and 1950's until the demise of Gas Lamps.

Hugh Wilson was the Lamplighter for several years before Mr Lauder in the 1930's and 1940's and he was subject to an unfortunate episode when he fell on a Lamplighters spike when putting out lamps only for it to go right through his face. The villages' Dr Houston was sent for, and he stitched his face while he lay on the kitchen table, with only swigs of whisky for anaesthetic.

Telephone

The *National Telephone Exchange Company* had Linwood connected to their system on Saturday the 24th of September 1886. Several of the public works in the district, including the *Clippens Oil Company*, were connected by wire.

Housing: Timeline of the Construction of Linwood Houses

Bridge Street and Napier Street were built in 1792 when Linwood officially came into existence. Buildings were added and replaced in these two streets, with Burnbrae Terrace, Holm Terrace, Lee Place, and Armour Place added in the early 20th Century. This was the way it was until the 1960 when it was announced that Linwood would be massively expanded to accommodate the new Car Plant and that housing and amenities would be needed for the incoming workers and their families.

Below is a chronological list of the housing developments of Linwood through its history.

Estate / Development / Road	Year	Estate / Development / Road	Year
Napier & Bridge Streets	1792	The East Fulton catchment areas was ready for occupancy in.	1970
Redan Rows Village	1855	Speirs/Semple/Holm places	1970
Inkerman Village	1856	North Clippens	1971
Balaclava Village	1856	Millford Drive, Melrose Avenue, Belmar and Asbury Courts	1973
Blackstoun Village	1840's	Greenhill Crescent and Drive	1976
Three villas on B.O.W. Road	1914	First Mentally Handicapped in UK housing - Erskinefauld Road	1980
Cottage flats on B.O.W. Road	1921	Mill Place	1980's
Hart Street and Dunlop Street	1934	Napier Garden	1985
Fulwood Avenue	1940	Lindon Gate	1993
Green Farm Road, Blackstoun/Moss/Watson Avenues	1940's	Cochrane Square	1996
Cotton Avenue Prefabs	1946	Stirling Gate.	2003
Pearson Place, Reid & Lochhead Avenues	1949	Muirhead / Stirling Drives	2005
Shaw Place	1953	Ryewraes Road	2007
New Car Plant announced	1960	Machrie Crescent	2014
The catchment areas of Abernethy/Cowal/Stirling/Lauder Drives, Kintyre Avenue, Erskinefauld & Brediland Roads	1964	Galbraith Drive	2022
Village Shopping Centre Flats	1971	Napier Grove	2023

Roads & Streets

Napier and Bridge Streets were created for the new village in 1792. However, there wasn't much else in the way of roads then apart from farmers dirt tracks. Those that did exist around Linwood then where: Candren Road; Bridge of Weir Road; Middleton Road; Moss Road; Clippens Road; Darluith Road; and Barochan Road.

Napier Street was named after Mr. William Napier, one of the three original owners of the Cotton Mill, and therefore founder of Linwood, and who afterwards became laird of Blackstoun.

The origin of the 'Clippens' road name, coming from Clippens House at the top of it, was formerly Clippings, and is thought to be derived from the time when the monks of Paisley Abbey allowed the local people to cut or clip the surrounding fields.

Roads and Streets were added throughout the 20th century with initial gradual growth in the early part, and rapid growth of estates from around 1962 onwards with creation of the *Rootes* Car Plant that would open in 1963. They were mainly named after former fine upstanding pillars of the community, business-owners and landowners, the likes of Middleton and Green Farm Roads after nearby farms, and some simply after places elsewhere in Scotland.

The *Scotsman* reported on the 30th of November 1968 that a new dual carriageway had been opened the previous day by Joint Under-Secretary of State for Scotland, Norman Buchan. The A737 Linclive Spur Link-Road would be a vital link in a multi-million-pound road complex linking Renfrewshire, Ayrshire, Dunbartonshire, Glasgow, Greenock and Edinburgh. At this time the A737 linked Linwood and Linwood Road to the St James's Interchange, and from there to M8 motorway, east and west, and the nearby new international airport soon to be completed at Abbotsinch, Paisley.

It would be more than three decades later that the Linclive Spur Link-Road would be extended to Howwood with a new flyover over the Linclive Roundabout as part of the new Johnstone-Howwood Bypass in 1993, and the road given the number A737.

A new 'perimeter' road was added around 1972 to by-pass the village on the south-side from the new bridge over the river Black Cart through to the new housing estates recently built in the north-west of Linwood and beyond.

Buses Termini

From when a bus service first started running to Linwood from Paisley, until today, below are the locations through time of the various bus termini as the town grew and expanded.

Late 1920's: The 1st terminus was at Linwood Cross turning around via South Napier St from Bridge Street, late 1920's

July 1948: The 2nd terminus was on Bridge of Weir Road turning around between the entrances to Lochhead Avenue and Shaw Place.

1966: The 3rd and current terminus on Clippens Road adjacent to start of Brediland Road and was purpose built to allow for turning and parking.

Tolls/Turnpikes

There were several 'Check-Bar' Tolls or Turnpikes around Linwood in the 19th century, which were the property of the 'Road Trustees'.

These Tolls were situated at:

DeafHillock Toll – at junction of Barnsford Road and Bridge of Weir Road

Moss Toll – at junction of Middleton and Moss Roads
Fulwood to Linwood Moss – likely at Gryfe Bridge
Crosslee to Linwood Toll – at bridge of Locher Water
Barnsford to Linwood Toll – at junction of Daluith and Barnsford Road
Linwood to Paisley Toll – at junction of Linwood Road, Ferguslie and Main Road
Bridge of Weir Road - at Junction with Clippens Road

An annual rent was charged to the trustees and an example of such rents was reported in the Glasgow Herald on Monday the 24th of April 1848 as: Deafhillock £330, and Barnsford to Linwood £515.

In Scotland, tolls were first abolished by the Roads and Bridges (Scotland) Act 1878, which stated "all highways shall be open to the public free from tolls and other exactions"

Bridges

In 1776 the Cochrane family of Clippens House, built a stone 'Linwood Bridge' over the river Black Cart, thus linking up their Clippens Estate Road to Linwood Road, then on to Paisley. Bridge Street in Linwood was named this bridge. In 1892 the bridge was re-structured to widen it to accommodate more traffic and pedestrians as reported in the *Glasgow Herald* on the 10th of April 1891 as follows.

"At a County Council meeting a report was submitted on the proposed improvements of the Linwood Bridge. The report, which was from the surveyors, was to the effect that the best and cheapest method of effecting a substantial improvement would be to extend the present bridge an addition of 14 feet to the upper side by means of stone arch. This scheme gave a carriage way of 20 feet and a footway of 5 feet over the bridge which was considered sufficient for the requirements of the district. The probable cost would be £675. The report was approved of."

A new road traffic bridge was created on the southern side of the of old 1796 built bridge over the river Black Cart around 1972, to link up with traffic to and from the Car Plant, the A737 and the M8 beyond, with the newly built village by-pass road leading through to the new estates recently built in the west of Linwood and beyond.

Fulwood Bridge over the river Gryfe, is a 3-span stone-built bridge; wide centre span, and elliptical. It is flanked by semi-circular arches with "1821" dated on west side and centre. This bridge carries Moss Road (an unclassified public road) over the River Gryfe to the West of Birkenhead steading.

Shoogley Bridge

The *Paisley & Renfrewshire Gazette* reported on the 28th of September 1901 *that "a bridge was being constructed between Linwood and Elderslie. This was being done in order to create a shortcut between the two places, to facilitate communication and, perhaps, help to do away with much of the trespassing on this portion of the Railway which was so common some time ago".*

The same newspaper further reported on the 26th of April 1902 that *"the new bridge at Mill O'Cart seems to be serving a greater and more important purpose than it was originally intended for. It has solved the difficulty of a short-cut from Linwood to Johnstone....".*

It would therefore seem that this bridge would have been the first 'shoogley' pedestrian bridge to be erected where previously there had only been stepping stones.

The *Paisley Daily Express* reported on the 11th of May 1928 that a meeting of the sub-committee on Roads, of the County of Renfrew, took place where funds where funds sought for *"the erection of a Bridge over the Black Cart water near the stepping-stones near to the Mill O' Cart Farm, Linwood"*, as the *"bridge would prove of considerable value in opening up traffic for unemployed persons"*. It is therefore likely that a replacement bridge was built shortly after this.

Not surprisingly, the 'Shoogley' bridge obtained its unofficial, but universally known name because it shoogled as one walked across it due to it rather flimsy design consisting of two I-Beam girders covered with slats, suspended over a considerable span of flowing water. It would often be covered in water when the river was in spate. The bridge fell into disrepair over the years and was replaced by another alongside it in the early 1990's. The new bridge also shoogles somewhat and the old bridge is still there in partial ruins but is fenced off to prevent use.

The Shoogley Bridge marks the border with Johnstone, near Elderslie, and on occasions in the 1960's/70's was the scene of pitched battles between Johnstone's 'Border' gang and Linwood's 'Paka' gang, although there weren't many accounts of serious injuries received or inflicted.

Over the 19th and 20th centuries there were many accounts in the newspapers of both accidental and suicide drownings, especially at the time when there was only stepping stones there.

The Lade and its Bridges

There were two bridges built over the Lade, either side of the Mill O'Cart farm, and this would have been at the time of the opening of the Cotton Mill, which the Lade served. One of those bridges connected the foot of Clippens Road with the stepping-stones , and later 'shoogley bridge, over the river Black Cart.

Fulwood Bridge, River Gryfe, is a 3-span stone-built bridge; wide centre span, and elliptical. This bridge carries Moss Road over the Gryfe to the West of Birkenhead steading.

Old [River Black] Cart 'Linwood Bridge': built in 1776 and remains in use today. A new wider bridge was built to replace it in 1972 due to the expansion of Linwood and its traffic.

Pre-1990 ruined 'Shoogley' Bridge as seen in 2023.

Blackstoun Bridge circa 2023

Town Centre Development, Shopping Centres and other Shops

The architect Sir Basel Spence, infamous for the *Hutchensontown C* atrocity in the redeveloped Gorbals in Glasgow, proposed very different plans for the new Linwood back in 1963, from those that were finally delivered.

The *Sir Basil Spence Archive* holds one manuscript batch for this project, which includes correspondence and written proposals outlining the design scheme and detailing its financial requirements. The material suggests the reasons why the small village of Linwood was ripe for developing into a small town; its proximity to the new *Rootes* Car Factory and *Pressed Steel* Plant foresaw an almost 100% rise in population over a 12-month period between 1963 and 1964. A decided lack of commercial facilities meant that Linwood was little prepared to cater for such an influx.

The manuscript material also shows that Spence considered the physical features of the site: the Mill Lade, lined by largish trees, and the slag heaps offered a superb opportunity to create a shopping centre with unique surroundings. His proposals were to include a series of shop frontages set back in stages to conform with the line of the Lade which was itself spanned by a series of wide bridges. Unfortunately. there are no drawings or photographs in the Archive.

In 1963, Glasgow based chartered surveyors, *James Barr and Son*, were working with a large London property company, *Regents Park Land Company Ltd*, who were interested in developing the centre of Linwood in Renfrewshire. Sir Basil Spence was asked to act as design consultant for the project architects, initially *Messer's Schingler Risdon Associates* and later *Fitzroy Robinson & Partners*. The design was for an inward-looking scheme, centred on the landscaped Mill Lade: a canal built to power the mill. It included a series of shopping precincts, a bowling alley, public house, dance hall and hotel as well as residential accommodation and amenity facilities. The team were unsuccessful in their proposals and instead, in July 1964, *Renfrew County Council* offered the redevelopment of *Linwood to City Wall Properties Ltd*.

The following year details of the new development were reported in the *Scotsman* on the 07th of July 1964. £3 million were to be spent on development plans for a vast new town and shopping centre at Linwood and these plans were approved in principle by *Renfrew County Council*. It was to include a town square, reserved for pedestrians, a 40-bedroom hotel with revolving restaurant, a bowling alley, possibly a swimming pool and parking facilities for 1000 cars. They planned three eight storey blocks of 150 houses with shops 'underneath. ' The new town centre would be sited between the present village and the *Rootes* car factory to the west of a motorway being built to link up with the new airport at Abbotsinch and a proposed bridge over the Clyde at Erskine. The Scottish Special Housing Association had been asked to assist in the house-building programme. The county council also agreed in principle to instruct a London company — the *City Wall Properties, Ltd*. — to carry out the development.

A photo of a model of the developers proposed layout of the new Linwood town and shopping centre –circa 1964.

The Tweedie Halls circa 1980's, was the biggest building in the Regional Shopping Centre and centre of the community.

Many of the developer's proposed amenities weren't delivered, notably the number of tower blocks [partly due to old mine-workings], the swimming pool, the bowling alley, and the hotel and restaurant, although the Golden Pheasant hotel would open nearby in 1967.

The revamped town and shopping centre finally opened in 1971 and was sold as Scotland's first regional shopping centre. It included the Tweedie Halls, Doctors Clinic, library, shop units with flats above them, post office, supermarkets, banks and major shops retailers such as Woolworths, Galbraiths-Cochrane, and Clydesdale.

Chronological Timeline from the Development to the Demise of Linwood Regional Shopping Centre

Year	Development
1964	The design of the new Linwood Regional Shopping Centre by City Wall Properties (London) is approved in principle by the Renfrew County Council. Huge error is made by the Council on the location as it shall be based at a far corner [old village centre] of the new vastly expanded Linwood Town, instead of the new centre around Clippens area.
1967	The new Linwood Regional Shopping Centre is under construction
1969	Linwood Regional Shopping Centre Construction is completed
1969	Slow uptake of the retail units delays the formal opening of the 'whole' centre
1971	Linwood Library opens
1971	The Commissioned Bronze Sculpture is unveiled in Ardlamont Square on 5th March
1971	The Opening of the Tweedie Halls by *Lord Lieutenant Viscount Muirsheil* and named after County District Clerk *Miss Tweedie* – 04th May
1971	Formal Opening of the new Clinic (had actually been opened since December 1970 – 22nd July
1971	The Opening of Woolworths by 1971 Miss Scotland *Libus Montgomery*- 11th August
1971	The Opening of Clydesdale (Electrics/Furniture) by singing duo *The Alexander Brothers* - end August
1971	The Opening of Galbraiths-Cochrane (Supermarkets) by singing duo *The Alexander Brothers* - end August
1971	The Opening of Regional Shopping Centre by County Convenor Dr J. McFarlane – 10th September
1971	The Banks, Post Office and other shops open, including Dominic's Fish n Chip Shop

1975	Half of the 50 retail units are still empty, so Council offers 2 years free rent to retailers
1981	The Car Plant Closes in May, and with it, unemployment rises greatly and so disposable income decreases, and Linwood population falls
1981	Over next three decades shops close and the shopping centre decays.
1991	Asda supermarket opened at the Phoenix Retail Park, thus contributing to the decline
2012	The Linwood Regional Shopping Centre is demolished – would be replaced by 'Tesco Town' opening at 8am on Thursday the 14th of August 2014.

During the demolition of the remaining old Linwood Parish Church Hall in 2010, a grim discovery was made by the workmen. They came across a crypt containing coffins, which after some enquiries turned out to be that of the Spiers family, formally of Blackstoun and Burnbrae houses. Then recollections of an old curse resurfaced. According to local legend, Lady Anne Speirs vowed disaster would devastate Linwood if the parish church where she lay buried was disturbed. It was said the prediction came true when the south Napier Street kirk was demolished in the 1970s and the town's car factory closed soon after, with hundreds of jobs lost.

However, the curse of Lady Anne Speirs has no factual basis. The doughty dowager had lived at Houston House and had no church or residential links with Linwood, and when she passed-away she was buried in Houston cemetery.

Tesco had hired a genealogist to trace the descendants of those buried. The mausoleum had been covered over in 1951 when the new church hall was constructed on the site. When the crypt was discovered, *Tesco* put a camera into the vault and established that there were four lead-lined coffins and debris which may be the remains of one or more wooden coffins. The firm believed the vault contained five members of the Speirs family

In 2010 *Tesco* has been given approval to exhume the 19th Century human remains before they could start demolition and then construction of the new shopping and town centre development. A judge granted an order allowing the firm to open a burial vault at the former parish church and remove the corpses for cremation or re-interment. *Tesco* had identified seventeen of their descendants and asked what their wishes were. The remains were duly reinterred following cremation at Whitekirk Churchyard in East Lothian, near the family home in North Berwick where R. T. N. Spier's eldest son Lt.-Col. Guy Thomas Spier, of 'The Abbel', North Berwick resided.

In December 2011 the Urban Realm magazine 'awarded' Linwood the "Plook on a Plinth" in the annual Carbuncle awards as being Scotland's most dismal town.

Midway through 2012 *Tesco's* contractors demolished the shopping centre; it had lasted 41 years. Construction of the new 8,100m2 superstore, shop units, a community centre, library and offices on the site, began shortly afterwards.

On the Thursday 14th of August 2014, after a seven-year wait, Linwood's multi-million-pound *Tesco* development was finally been unveiled. Bright and breezy shoppers poured through the doors of the 40,000 sq ft supermarket just before it started trading at 8am. Celebrations continued at 10am with a special ceremony, which saw local community champion Jeanette Anderson, and store manager Colin Caldow and his colleagues, cut a ribbon to declare the official opening. Local hero Jeanette, who was chairwoman of *Linwood Community Development Trust*, was nominated for the privilege by her daughter Jacqueline Thompson, as a reward for her tireless contribution in making Linwood a brighter, better place.

Clippens Small Shopping Centre

An advert in the *Scotsman* newspaper on the 13th of May 1963, by the SSHA, were details of a Tender for new shops at a small shopping centre at Clippens Road. The advert said that the SSHA *"propose to provide shops to service a population of about 4700 at the above scheme"*.

Another advert by SSHA in the same newspaper on the 07th of September, in the same year, was a tender for a shop that would act as a newsagents, tobacconist, confectioner, and possibly sub-post office. After several years of trading, this shop would be run from 1980 to 2010 by Jimmy Doyle and his wife Lynn, who were an integral party of the community, and were well known.

Once let, this small shopping centre consisted of the Newsagents, Starks Chemist, the Dairy and a Galbraiths grocery shop. From the onset of the 21st century the shop units became empty and the whole area generally run-down, with only the Shopping Basket grocery shop still in business by 2023, albeit under a different owner.

Other Supermarkets

The *Co-op* had a shop on the west end of Bridge Street for many years during the 20th Century. After being demolished in the late 1960's, it was re-built as the Co-op, but later became *Shoprite*, *Kwik-Save*, and had several other uses including as a snooker club and charity shop. In the early years of the *Linwood Regional Shopping Centre*, it had supermarkets such as *Galbraiths-Cochrane*, *Templeton's*, *Presto*, *Pick-n-Save*, and the later *The Orchard*.

Jessie Mackies (Carrol's / Vince's) Shop

Starting off as *'Jessie Mac's'* in the early 1950's, it was initially not much more than a shed, but would later expand into average size grocery and general provisions shop. It would prove invaluable to many Linwoodonians as it was often the only place opened on a Sunday. In the 1970's there was a fad for using Paraffin heaters and this shop was the place to get your Paraffin. It later changed hands and became *Carrol's*, then *Vince's*, and then several more reincarnations and is today called *Greenfarm Market*.

Phoenix Retail Park

In November 1991 Asda supermarket opened at the Phoenix Retail Park on the outskirts of Linwood at the site of the old car plant. It was soon followed by many other shops, restaurants, a hotel, a cinema, several car showrooms. This would become the main place for Linwood people to shop and so contributed to the decline of the Linwood Regional Shopping Centre.

Door to Door Salesmen

From 1947 until around 1970 door-to-door salesmen of either Indian or Pakistan heritage, would come round the doors of Linwood selling their wears out of a suitcase. Typical items included nylon stockings, hair ribbons, and shoe laces, in the earlier days, and then brushes, cloths, and mop heads in later years. Apparently one of them went one to be a millionaire owner of one of the large cash n carry shops up in Glasgow's south side.

Galbraith's Stores Limited

William Galbraith was born in 1862 in Napier Street, Linwood, and for a while as a boy worked in his father John Galbraith's small grocery store (*Galbraith and Sons Ltd*) at No. 15 Napier Street. When he had grown up into his teens, he went to get experience in the trade in Glasgow. He didn't stay there long as he had the ambition and initiative to own his own shop and this, he did in 1882 opening first shop in Sandholes in Paisley, the other shops were soon added and such was his success that Mr Galbraith established *Galbraith's Stores Limited* in 1894. By 1900 he was the proprietor of twelve stores and had expanded to over 59 shops by 1919. To minimise capital outlay the stores, usually located in Tenement Blocks, were rented, designed in a uniform style and had narrow shop frontages. It established its headquarters in Paisley with a warehouse in George Street and created its own bakeries, ham curers and tea blending establishments to supply its own shops. The store network grew rapidly, by 1939 the company had over 159 grocery branches and 12 butchers' shops. Along with a "provisions" window, staple items such as tea, sugar and bakery goods were advertised with the emphasis on price. By the time of the sale of the business to *Home and Colonial* in 1954 the store network had expanded to over 220 stores and was regarded as the leading independent grocery business in the west of Scotland. The company survived as a trading subsidiary of *Argyll Supermarkets* (along with *R & J Templeton*) until 1987.

Mr William Galbraith was a prominent personality in the Paisley district and had served as councillor and a magistrate. He passed away on the 29th of July 1945 at his home in *Larrieston*, Elderslie, aged 83.

Police Station

As reported in the *Paisley & Renfrewshire Gazette* on the 12th of May 1900, the first Police Station in Linwood opened on Bridge Street between Burnbrae Terrace and Lee Place in 1901. The second Police station opened in 1961 at the foot of Dunlop Street, and the old station was then demolished a little earlier. In the 1990's Police business was transferred to the Johnstone station and the Linwood station building lay disused for several years and eventually became a private dwelling.

Registrar's Office

A notice put in the *Paisley Daily Express* on Saturday the 16th of December 1882, informed the public that Linwood was to become its own district with defined boundaries encompassing Clippins and Blackstoun villages, for the purposes of registration act. It was also stated that this would take effect from the 01st of January 1883 when Mr James Mitchell, Schoolmaster, would take up the duties of district Registrar for Births, Death, and Marriages, at premises at No. 15 Napier Street.

Sports Facilities

The Sports Centre opened in 1978 and was well-equipped for most types of sports activities, and was utilised by local schools for Physical Education Lessons.

The centre was upgraded and in May 2013 Linwood's Sport and Community Centre *ON-X* formally opened following a £24m investment by Renfrewshire Council. It had been designed *by Cr8 Architecture* and built by *BAM Construction*. Facilities included an eight-court sports hall, two squash courts, 600sq m gym, four fitness studios, and athletics track. It also featured three swimming pools including a six-lane 25m competition pool, teaching pool and leisure pool with flumes and lazy river feature. The gym offers 100 stations, a functional training area and a dedicated indoor cycling studio. Outdoors a sand dressed floodlit pitch was available for seven and 11 a side football, as well as hockey, rounders and touch rugby.

Worship
Religious Tracts

The *Paisley Religious Tract Society* was the local branch of a *British Evangelical Christian Organisation* founded in 1799 in London and know for publishing a variety of popular religious and quasi-religious texts in the 19th Century, which they did for profit. Their aim was to provide Tracts that were plain, striking, entertaining, and adapted to various situations and condition of its audience. Their group members were drawn mainly from the protestant religions: Anglican, Presbyterian, Free High Church, and Baptist. From the 1830's and throughout the remainder of the 19th century these Tracts were distributed monthly to places such as the Paisley prison and army barracks, hospitals within the county, and the various Bleachfields in the neighbourhood, including those in the village of Linwood.

Even before Linwood had a parish church, efforts were being made to gather villagers on the sabbath for the purpose of worship. The *North British Daily Mail* reported on the 12th of March 1857, that *"About six or eight months ago an attempt was made to establish a preaching station in this popular village, there being no place of within worship within two miles of its inhabitants. At about the time we mention, the Rev. Mr Wallace, a probationer of the Paisley Presbytery, as appointed to work, and the results are all that could be desired. Mr Wallace having obtained the use of the village school-room, commenced his labours by visiting from house to house and inviting all those who chose to attend to meet him there on the sabbath. Gradually as the attendance upon his ministrations increased, and the earnest and eloquent preaching of Mr Wallace became more and more valued."*

Schooling was strongly linked with religion and worship, and this was demonstrated in an article in the *Paisley Herald and Renfrewshire Advertiser* on the 09th of July 1859, gives an overview of the state of schooling in the greater Linwood area at that *time*. This account comes from an "Ordinary monthly meeting of the Free Church Presbytery of Paisley" and goes like this.

"The Rev. Mr Dodds, of Dunbar, a member of deputation from the Home Mission Committee, made a short statement in reference to the operations of the deputation about Johnstone, Kilbarchan, Inkerman, Balaclava, and Linwood. They had been constantly engaged visiting from house to house, distributing tracts, and conversing with the people, in addition to preaching to the several villages in the open air. He had met with no interruption, there were on all occasions, good audiences — in some instances large—and those composing them generally listened with much attention. The field was too large for two deputies, but still he hoped much good would done. He had entered the houses of Latter-day Saints, as they were called, and Roman Catholics, and met with nothing but civility. In Inkerman and Balaclava there was a great want of education felt by the people. At Balaclava, out of a population of 110 children and youths, between the ages of five and sixteen years, there were only twenty at any school whatever, leaving ninety running about, either receiving no training, or a training to what was evil. Every mother and father almost—the Latter-Day Saints and Roman Catholics as well the Protestants—were most anxious for the getting up of a school at Balaclava, and steps were being taken to bring the matter before the proprietors of the works. At Inkerman the educational destitution was fully as great. There was a school, no doubt, at Linwood, but that school was barely sufficient for the children belonging to that village, and it was otherwise not desirable that the children at Balaclava and Inkerman should be required to go there. He believed the blessings and gratitude of all the parents would rest upon this Presbytery if they assisted in getting necessary schools. The work the deputation was engaged in was arduous and trying in some respects, but still he regarded it as particularly interesting. From what he had seen there was much need for greater concentration and unity of effort for the purpose of securing the spiritual welfare of a mass of their fellow men, who were gradually sinking deeper and deeper into a state of spiritual destitution." Mr Fraser added that *"the villages of Balaclava and Inkerman were scarcely completed, and the people themselves, under the direction of their managers, who must be better acquainted with the circumstances than the Presbytery."*

So, we can see that education was strongly linked to religion and that there was belief that not being educated would lead individuals into *"spiritual destitution"* and that non-religious teachings could be *"evil"*. We can also see that only 18% of children at this time attended the schools [many were called 'sabbath' schools] that were provided by their fathers' employers; companies such as *Messrs Merry and Cunningham Ltd.*, who owned several mines in the area. Perhaps this was due to lack of affordability of children to attend school, or maybe also because some of the older ones were working themselves.

Linwood Parish Church (Church of Scotland)

The foundation stone of Linwood Parish Church was laid by *Messer's Jeffrey Builders* of Johnstone on the 25th of June 1859, with the assistance of Brethren of local Masonic Lodges Kilbarchan, Johnstone and Lochwinnoch, who conducted the demonstration with many Linwood villagers in attendance.

The land for to the church was feud by Thomas Spiers Esquire., of Blackstone, to certain local trustees, in 1859, at a nominal feu-duty of one penny, and the property conveyed the general assembly deed on constitution.

Building work on the *Chapel of Ease* was completed and opened on the 12th of June 1860. The Rev. Mr. James Wallace was ordained as the first Minister of the church. The building, both as regards the interior and internally, done great credit to the taste and skill of James Wilson, Esq. of Blackstone House, who furnished the design. The building was seated for a congregation of about 500 persons, and the internal arrangements being convenient and comfortable. Ventilation was in place, and a heating apparatus was also to be provided. The external architectural effect being good, the building having character in the design, and forming quite an ornament to the village.

The manse was erected in 1873 on land that was fued-out by the Duke of Abercorn for £4 15s, located on the right-hand side, at beginning of Candren Road. The Rev. Mr. James Douglas (serving 1867-73) was its first tenant.

Linwood became a *quoad sacra* parish when it was constituted on the 19th of January 1880 in the presbytery of Paisley.

A new church hall was provided in 1951 at the cost of £6000, and sometime during that same decade the small Bell Tower was taken off by lighting and was never replaced.

Over a century later, in February 1965, the consecration stone for the current church building was laid at the new location on Clippens Road. The church includes a large aluminium cross presented by the former *Rootes Car Plant*, as well as a fine pipe organ from 1957. At the time of the publication of this book, the current church building was earmarked for closure and the parish to union with Elderslie Kirk to form a new parish, covering the whole collective area. And it was hope that there would still be a worship site for the Church of Scotland in Linwood, but that it may be a shared premises, with the church as a tenant.

The old church was then used for other community activities and storage. There was an attempt to sell both the church and hall in 1974 with adverts in newspapers, but they never sold. The church then had to be demolished in 1981 after falling into a state of disrepair, although the church hall remained until 2013 when it was demolished for the new Tesco and shopping centre being built in the village.

Other Ministers of note are as follows:

Rev Milne: Served from 1873 until 1880. Sadly, died on Christmas day 1883 with internal injuries after his horse had fallen on top of him the previous day.

Rev John Adamson Abernethy: Serving as Minister at Linwood from 1880-1926, he has been Linwood's longest serving clergyman ever, and after whom Abernethy Drive is named. He died in 1935 in Fairlie in Ayrshire.

Rev James C. Hill M.A.: Served from 1926 until retirement in 1953, he was the author of *'Linwood – Paisley and District'* (1953), the first book written about Linwood.

The Very Reverend Andrew Herron: He had been Minister at Linwood from 1936 until 1940 before moving to Houston, and later became the *Moderator for the General Assembly of the Church of Scotland* in 1971-72, retired in 1981, and passed away in 2003 in Giffnock at the age of 93.

Rev Colin Morton: Serving as Minister at Linwood from 1962 until 1973. He was born in China in 1933 to two missionary parents. He later married American academic Carol in 1961. The Rev Colin Morton baptised many of the incomer families' children in the 1960's and early 1970's, including this author, and his wife ran a nursery in Linwood. He died on the 16th of June 2011, in Edinburgh, aged 77.

Rev Jack Drummond: Serving as Minister at Linwood from 1973 until 1986, before moving on to Rutherglen. He well known to many of us in the 1970's and 1980's, often visiting schools. He retired in 2013

St Conval's Roman Catholic Church (Candren Road)

The spread of Catholicity in the Linwood district and the whole of the West of Scotland in second half of the 19th Century was quite rapid. This was due to the incoming workers and their families from Ireland looking for work and to settle, as Ireland was bereft of opportunities and had suffered its great potato famine. Churches and schools sprung up in places where in former years some solitary brick building represented both church and school, and in the country the increase, though not so marked, was nevertheless equally certain. Linwood, itself just a little village consisting of just two streets, had the neighbouring hamlets of Clippens, Blackstoun, and Inkerman, where many Irish had settled and worked. However, the district which formerly employed large numbers of men in the mining industry, pits closing down one-by-one, had become stagnant, and the area which had given such original promise, had declined terribly in the late 19th Century.

Up until the year 1898 Linwood had been served from Johnstone, and Mass was then celebrated in a humble little chapel-school. In that year the Diocesan authorities, recognising the difficulty of the district being properly served from Johnstone, and so decided to create a new mission, and therefore, the new St Conval's Parish was founded in 1898 to serve the Local Catholic Community of Linwood and its surrounds.

Linwood was accordingly separated from Johnstone, and Rev. Father Shaw was appointed its first pastor. A somewhat difficult charge, it could have been placed in no better hands. A widely scattered parish, including hamlets long distance from the main village, organisation was extremely difficult, and at the commencement it was a decidedly uphill fight.

An ordinance Survey map of 1900 shows an R.C. Church at a little side road just off Blackstoun Road, near Boghead Farm. The church, called St. Milburga, had been there since 1896 and was a small and simple wooden structure. It was there to serve the hamlets of Blackstoun and Inkerman, but it would soon be dismantled and moved it to a site at the Linwood end of Candren Road, where it would be re-assembled and incorporated as part of a new church.

All difficulties were overcome, and the new church was built, and on the 06th of May, 1906, under the episcopate of Archbishop John McGuire, the new parish of St Conval was opened. There had been a Public Notice put in Glasgow Observer and Catholic Herald the previous day advertising for a *"Solemn Opening of the new Church"* the following day with a 1s admission charge.

The fact that Father Shaw had been able to build a church and procure a cottage presbytery is sufficient in itself. The church was a picturesque little building of wood with a stone foundation, and seated accommodation for over 400. It was adorned with a somewhat simple, a but beautiful High Altar, and two side altars dedicated to the Blessed Virgin and the Sacred Heart. A little space was reserved at the back of the church for-the choir.

There was a large and representative congregation at the opening ceremony on Sunday. Solemn High Mass was celebrated by Very Rev. Provost Chisholm, Father Walsh, 'Paisley. being deacon, and Father McIntyre, Johnstone, sub-deacon, Father Young, Paisley, was master of ceremonies. After the first Gospel, Very Rev. Father Meany, St Mary's cathedral, Aberdeen, delivered the opening sermon. Taken as his text the words *"They shall be inebriated with the plenty of God's House"*.

In 1930 Father Dennehy came to Linwood and recognised the need for creating a larger, more permanent structure. Two years later the new St Conval's church was completed in its current situation, beside the older wooden church which would from then on be used as the church hall. Then, on the 06th of November 1932, with solemn ceremony, the new church of St Conval's was blessed and opened by Archbishop MacKintosh.

St Conval's Roman Catholic Church (Green Farm Road)

By the mid-1960's Linwood had grown rapidly with thousands new families moving to Linwood to settle due to the work opportunities at the new Car Plant. The Catholic population had grown from 3,100 in an estimated total population at the time of 11,000, and therefore a bigger, and newer, church, was required. A suitable site was identified at the corner of Green Farm and B.O.W. Roads, that had previously been occupied by 'The Farm of Green' since the late 17th century, but had recently been demolished.

On Monday the 12th of September 1966, a ceremony was held to mark the laying of the new St Conval's Church, and work got underway. Friday 02nd of June 1967, Feast of the Sacred Heart, the first Mass was held at the newly opened church by Bishop Black.

The new church had seated accommodation for 624 persons in the nave and 36 persons in the choir gallery. Unusually for a Catholic Church, it contained a War Memorial, there being no Civic Centre in Linwood when the Parish was established. And the Chrysler car plant had donated the metal for the cross in the church.

When this new church opened, the old church built in 1932 was soon converted to St Conval's Social Club.

On the 23rd of December 1974 Police diverted traffic away from the church after the 80-foot Bell Tower (with heavy metal cross and bell) began to lean 2-foot from its perpendicular and experts who examined it said that it would have to be demolished. However, just before its planned demolition one week later on the 30th, the tower collapsed exactly along the line of the path planned by the demolition team, thus saving them a job. The only damage was to a railing, and some of the debris was thrown into the 'wee red school'.

Other Priests of note are as follows:

Rev Hugh Chisolm: Served St Margaret's Parish in Johnstone from 1859, but whose zeal and diligence was responsible for establishing a Chapel-School in Napier Street.

Rev Daniel Gillon: Served 1910-1915, until his passing: He was responsible for obtaining the old Linwood Public School building in 1911 and adding it to the current St Conval's school, and completely refurbishing and equipping it accordingly.

Rev William Molloy: Served 1928-1930. He was responsible for partly demolishing and re-building the school in Napier Street.

Very Reverend James Canon Fisher: Served from 1964 to 1977, until his passing. He was the priest that most of the incomers to Linwood will remember best from their youth.

The Gospel Hall

Influenced by the Religious Revival in the UK in 1904, initially a small number of Christians broke away from established churches and started meeting in a local community centre that same year. They then built and opened Linwood Gospel Hall in 1908. They later added and extension in 1974/75 and changed the layout. The Gospel Hall remains in the same location today. This revival had begun as an effort to kindle non-denominational, non-sectarian spirituality, the revival had coincided with the rise of the labour movement, socialism, and a general disaffection with religion among the working class and youths. The movement had spread to Scotland and England, with estimates that a million people were converted throughout Britain. Profanity was so diminished in the coal mines that the pit-ponies dragging the coal carts in the tunnels did not understand their commands anymore and stood still, confused.

A few Episcopalians also lived in the village and worshipped in St. Johns Church in Floors Street in the nearby town of Johnstone.

Balaclava

The *Glasgow Herald* reported that during a meeting of the *Established Church Presbytery* in Paisley on the 03d of February 1875, there was a proposal for *"erecting an iron church at Balaclava as the centre of the mining district, several members maintaining that all the people who attended church in these villages either went a to Johnstone or Paisley. The question was remitted back to the committee for reconsideration, and to report."* However, this was not rea ised.

Education

Below is chronological timelines of schools in the Linwood district

State / Presbyterian / Non-Denominational Schools

Year	School Developments
1792	Linwood Mill School Opens (aka 'half-time school').
1855-1939	Inkerman Works or Public School was established for children of the miners and brickyard workers. Here the pupils were taught 'the 3 R's', History, Geography, Bible Knowledge and Latin. With the demolition of village in 1939, families were moved to Linwood and Elderslie, and so children attended schools there.
1862 - 1877	Clippens and Balaclava Sabbath or Public and Industrial School – until Linwood Public School opened in 1877 when pupils transferred there. It was established for children of the miners and shale oil workers
1877	Linwood Public School in Napier Street opens (extended in 1884 at cost of £300)
1911	Linwood Public School moves to new building in Bridge of Weir Road (Wee Red School)
1964	Craigends Primary School Opens
1965	Linwood High School Opens (later demolished in 2006)
1965	Mossedge Primary School Opens
1969	East Fulton Primary School Opens
1988	Mossedge merges with/at Craigends to become Woodlands Primary School
2007	Woodlands Primary School rebuilt/opens
2008	Linwood High School opens after being rebuilt

Roman Catholic Chapel and State Schools

Year	School Development
1865	R.C. / Chapel School in Napier Street
1911	St Convals' School takes over building vacated by Linwood Public School in Napier Street
1964	St Brendans Primary / High School Opens
1969	St Conval's Primary School Opens
1972	St Andrews Primary School Opens
1988	Our Lady of Peace becomes new name for St Andrews
1988	St Conval's Primary School closes and is demolished soon afterwards
2006	St Benadict's High School Opens

St Conval's R.C. Church / School – circa 1900.

St Conval's [formerly Linwood Public] School – circa 1963.

Linwood Public [Wee Red] School – circa 1970's

East Fulton Primary School - circa 2017

1964 photo of St Brendan's Primary / Secondary School; when it opened the old Railway line was still in-place.

Linwood High School entrance in 2006 just before it was demolished and a new one replaced it same name.

As early as 1864 a basic education was provided in the village at the Inkerman Works School by Teacher Andrew Ross. The school, situated a short distance from the village on the Candren Road to Linwood, and still stands today, but used a residency. Neighbouring Blackstoun hamlet had a similar such school.

On the 16th of January 1892, the *Paisley & Renfrewshire Gazette* reported census of children recorded at a School Board Meeting, thus: *"the Clerk submitted following figures: — Total children attending school, 508—of* whom 330 were Protestant and 158 Roman Catholic; of the Protestant children, 250 were enrolled in Linwood Public School, the remaining 93 attending Inkerman, Johnstone, &c."

Tragically, as reported in the *Paisley & Renfrewshire Gazette* on the 22nd of April 1899, the body of 50-year-old Mr. James Mitchell, Headmaster of Linwood Public School, had been found in the Lade near the Paper Mill: "Mr Mitchell had been depressed for some time, and just the week before a temporary teacher had been put in charge until his recovery."

The same newspaper reported on the 03rd of October 1908 that Evening continuation classes had again been opened at Linwood Public School: "Fifty pupils (36 girls and 16 boys) enrolled under the supervision of Mr Mathew Mycroft. Drawing and Machine Construction, English, Cookery, and Needlework are being taught. Many young men are debarred from Linwood evening school owing to their late hours at work. It is an unusual fact this season that no Roman Catholics have joined."

Neglection of Children's Education

Education wasn't always amongst the first priorities of some parents and employers. One example of this was reported in the *Paisley & Renfrewshire Gazette* on the 05th of May 1883: "Arthur McArthur, Carter, Linwood, was summoned to appear at the same Court, but failed to appear, and a warrant was granted for his apprehension. McArthur was brought up before the Court on Thursday, and pleaded guilty of neglecting to educate his children, explaining that he left home early in the morning, and could not see personally whether his children attended school. The Sheriff informed him he was responsible even although he expected his wife should see that the children attended school, and fined him in 10s, with 20s. expenses."

Another example was reported in the same newspaper on the 16th of November 1907: "At a meeting of the School Board, it was heard that a child was kept from school because he hadn't any clothes to wear, and this even though the father was earning 30s a week. Most of the money was spent upon drink. No adequate law for dealing with such a case seemed to exist at this time. The board also heard the case of two other truant boys were upon the books because neighbouring farmers (who ought to have known better) had hired them to work in their fields."

And employers were sometimes guilty of abusing the system by employing cheap labour. The *Glasgow Citizen* reported on the 02nd of March 1844 that "the Linwood [Cotton Spinning] Company had been prosecuted for the following infringements of the 'Factories Regulation Act' namely, for employing children in their work under thirteen years of age, without certificate of age and school attendance; also, for neglecting to enter their children's names in the register of workers and time register; and being convicted of those offences, they were found liable in penalties to the amount of three guineas, besides costs."

The following is a first-hand account of the experiences of a Linwood education during the middle 20th Century, as told by Betsy Brennan:

"I attended St. Conval's school from 1955 until 1962. It was a mixed-sex School and I attend ½ day until after Christmas then for the full day starting at 9am until 4pm. We had to stand in line outside until we were called to the sound of the hand-held school bell ringing, first line was Primary 1, then all classes went in this order all the way to Primary 7. It was separate playgrounds for boys and girls. Teachers stood at the classroom door and the girls had to curtsey and the boys had to salute the teacher, before entering class room, then once seated we had to stand for morning prayers, which were also said before lunch break, after lunch break, and at home-time. Subjects were mostly the '3 Rs' and catechism, with occasional painting lessons, spelling tests and writing essays. Gym was once a week, and it was in your bare feet, and Navy-blue knickers; I cannot remember if the boys had a separate gym period or not. One thing I do remember is one of the girls wearing navy blue knickers had a pocket in them, wow, really fancy, I remember thinking what the hell use would it be, I mean if you kept a hankie there it would mean you had to lift your skirt to retrieve it; if you needed to blow your nose. There were music lessons and it was Percussion instruments such as: Tambourines, triangles and one that you had to clack (cannot remember the name). Friday afternoon after lessons ended was assembly where Miss Glen gave a speech about what had happened over the week."

Corporal Punishment

Corporal punishment in the 18th and 19th Centuries consisted of the Tawse (leather thong belt, or strap) if you were lucky, and the Cane and the Ferule if you were not, the latter being 'a flat wooden ruler with a widened end - used for beating children'.

To get an insight into corporal punishment in the early 20th Century we can refer to this excerpt from a letter to the Editor of the *Paisley & Renfrewshire Gazette* on the 07th of December 1901 from a section headed 'LINWOOD':

"A case came under our notice which I thought ought to have been taken into Court, where probably the teacher would have been taught a lesson which, for some time at any rate, would save other children from such punishment. To an alarming extent some teachers are in the habit of slapping children about the head and face, while punching them in the sides and back is, apparently, a part of their daily programme. Parents have a just cause of complaint; but complaining to the teachers is simply like throwing water on a duck's back. The members of the School Board are responsible to the electors, and the sooner some of the members of the various Boards take up the question the more credit it will be to them. There is no denying the fact that in some schools, things are going to extremes. It is also a fact that some of the members of the School Boards know what is going on, yet they "sing dumb." But there is a day of reckoning in the future when these things will be brought to light."

I, myself went to Linwood High School from 1976-81 and received 'the belt', sometimes 'six of the best', for my misbehaviour, and I probably deserved most of the time. It was best to shut your eyes, brace yourself, and just take what was coming, because if you pulled away slightly and the belt only got your fingers instead of palm and fingers, the teacher would apply the strap more times. So, you could end up getting 8 or 9 hits and it was all you could do to put your affected hand under a cold running tap to relieve the pain.

From the start of the 1982 spring term, no child was ever belted again, just 9 months after I left high school. The Education Act (No 2) Act 1986 finally banned corporal punishment and, in August 1987, became law. It was over.

There was also a form of indirect punishment when I went to school, primary and high schools. If you got a letter sent home to your parents because of your misbehaviour, you risked getting a 'doing' of your father when he got home and read it, or even worse, being 'kept in' [grounded] for a week.

Since 1982 until today, detention has been the main punishment given out to pupils, which restricts their freedom to mix with their friends after school.

Transport

In a letter written to a newspaper, dated 22nd of November 1895, Renfrew County Provost Buskin had the following to say about Linwood under the title *"Our Best Suburb"*:

"The railway facilities are extremely generous, within the village there are two goods stations, while the passenger stations of Elderslie. Johnstone. and Houston are each at the convenient distance of about 2 & ½ miles away. As there are no conveyances to any of these stations, and the various roads to them are without the slightest shelter."

Horses & Omnibuses

Horse drawn omnibuses were the main form of public transport in the 19th and early 20th Centuries. These would run to Paisley and Johnstone from where the public could link up with trains. Horses would also pull gigs, cabs and carriages as forms of transport during this period. And horses were used to pull carts of cargo in business for delivery to customers.

The *Paisley & Renfrewshire Gazette* reported on the 08th of April 1899, that *"Parliament would be by the Parish Council to provide a subsidy in order to maintain a bus service between Linwood and Elderslie Station."*

In Linwood there was a large grassy wasteland to the south of Bridge Street up until 1973 when the Greenhill Estate started to be built. It was known locally as 'Horses Park', and presumably got its name because it was used for working horses to graze and exercise, back in the early 19th Century. This area was also used for the 'Shows' (Funfair) in the 1960's/70's.

Railway

Since the *Glasgow & South Western Railway's* line from Glasgow via Paisley (Canal station) to Greenock opened in 1869, which bypassed Linwood near its western border, Linwood had made many attempts for a new station for its people. For many years the nearest stations were Elderslie and Houston & Crosslee, which were both around 3 miles walk from Linwood village. The Linwood area already had several spur lines, but these were used by the mining companies and mills and were for transporting their minerals and goods only. There were also two Goods Yards, one at the corner of Bridge Street and Moss Road, the other to the south-east side if Linwood Parish Church.

On the 26th of November 1872, the *Glasgow Herald* reported that Parliamentary notice had been given of three railways to be made in connection with the Glasgow and South-Western Railway at and near to Johnstone. One of them was *"for the construction, of which powers are sought, is proposed to commence by a junction with the Bridge of Weir Railway at a point a about a hundred and seventy yards in an easterly direction from the farm-steading of Muirhead, on the south side of the turnpike road to Linwood, occupied by Mr Thomas Rutherford, and terminating three hundred and ten yards in a south-westerly direction from Linwood House, occupied by Mr George Ronaldson. This railway is intended to accommodate the inhabitants of Linwood, who have long complained of the want of railway facilities for the conveyance of goods and passengers."*

On January the 17th 1874, the *Paisley Herald and Renfrewshire Advertiser* reported that Linwood village, *"will, it is understood, soon be connected with the Greenock & Ayrshire Railway, by the formation of a branch starting from a point near the Mill o' Cart, on the Greenock section of the line. The Surveyors sere on the ground this week, and a set of plans which have been prepared, show that the line of route places the terminus near the village of Linwood, just in the centre of lands abounding in minerals."*

There are many other examples of reports promising a railway station at Linwood over the years, all of which proved to be promises broken.

On the 19th of July 1971, the *Scotsman* reported that a Linwood campaign group had renewed their plea to *"persuade British Rail to build a station to serve the growing township of Linwood. About 15 passenger trains a day travel between Glasgow Central and Kilmacolm, passing the western perimeter of Linwood. But the town's residents travelling to Glasgow have to go by bus to Paisley, and then catch another bus or a train. Three years ago, British Rail rejected a request to build a halt at Linwood".*

Tramway

Tramways were built in the late 19th Century, but the nearest they ran to Linwood was past the West [Linwood] Toll. The Linwood public complained and there was a movement in the 1880's/90's to get the company to extend a line to Linwood, but to no avail.

Buses

Graham's Buses began running services from Linwood to Hawkhead in Paisley in 1932, to Govan Cross in 1959, and to Houston in 1969. In 1977, Greater Glasgow PTE sponsored a "Linwood Clipper" service, worked jointly by Grahams and Western SMT, which ran from Linwood to central Glasgow Anderston Bus Station via the M8 motorway. For a time, Grahams also participated in the Kilmacolm to Glasgow "Link Line" services following the elimination of train services in January 1983, but later withdrew from the routes.

Sadly, Graham's buses ceased trading at midnight on the 29th April 1990. Strathclyde buses took over the services and hired some of the drivers. Later McGill's buses would take over the services and still operate them today.

Graham's buses are still badly missed today as everyone knew what a reliable service they provided over many years, a standard that subsequent services have failed to live up to.

Aviation

A strange flying incident was reported in the *Paisley Daily Express* on the 17th of May 1926 which occurred near Houston & Crosslee Railway Station the previous Friday afternoon, when *"a mail-carrying aeroplane came to grief. The pilot, bound for Renfrew Aerodrome, having lost his direction, volplaned close to the ground and shouted to two road workers below — "Renfrew?". The whirr of the propeller naturally prevented the roadmen from hearing the airman's appeal, but the village postman, some distance away, clearly heard the call but was not spotted by the pilot, who lifted his machine into the air and elected to land. The difference, at this season, between a cornfield and pasture land seemingly cannot be realised from the skies, and the aviator struck a bad patch and landed in a field of shooting corn, and, naturally, in the soft going, his machine went "head-over-heels". The airman had come out of the ordeal without the proverbial scratch despite his rough-and-tumble throw on landing. On appealing to a passing motor-car owner, the pilot, with the mail aboard, was soon speeding through Linwood for Renfrew Aerodrome. After disposing of his mail-bags, the airman returned to Houston & Crosslee Station by motorcar, took his camera from the plane and took a photograph. An aircraft break-down squadron removed the damaged aeroplane later in the afternoon, and quietness again reigned on the countryside."*

It was reported in the Sunday Mail newspaper on the 28th of August 1927 that *Berkshire Aviation Tours* company was offering to the public to *"See Paisley by Air"*. The company had acquired a temporary makeshift airstrip for one week only at a field at Barskiven Farm – just of Linwood Road, and you could get a flight for 5 shillings.

Tragedy struck when a Cessna 404 light aircraft with eleven on board crashed minutes after take-off near Blackstone Farm, just outside Linwood on the 03rd of September 1999, killing eight people. Mr John Connell, a landscape worker working nearby at Middleton Farm heard one of the aircraft's twin engines fail before it went down and went to the scene on a tractor and saw a bloodied Airtours pilot crawling from the wreckage. He dragged the pilot and a steward clear of the flames before rescuing another flight attendant who was still strapped in his seat. Mr Connell's actions saved the lives of Captain Hugh O'Brien and his colleagues, Keven MacKenzie and Derek Morrison. Eight people, including five air stewardesses and an Airtours pilot, died in the tragedy which happened as the plane took nine Airtours staff to Aberdeen to catch a charter flight to Majorca.

Months after the accident, Mr Connell was given a British Red Cross humanity award for his action, and was also presented with the Queen's bravery award.

Emigration and Culture

In its formative years the people of Linwood village were employed mostly in Cotton Mill. They had a simple existence, where God fearing people, and went to church once per week, which at this period would have been in Johnstone. At this time the population would have been predominantly protestant in faith, but then came the Irish who came for the work opportunities. This is a very important point as culture comes from where one is brought up, and from one's religion, and this would have a large impact on the collective culture of Linwood going forward,

In his book *'The Industries of Scotland: Their Rise, Progress and Present Condition'* (1869) - Coal Mining section, author David Bremner tells of how the incoming Irish workers were viewed by native Protestant Scots, which may well come across as offensive with today's viewpoint:

"The rapid development of the coal and iron trades in the west of Scotland led to an immense influx of Irish labourers between 1830 and 1850; and as they were generally very ignorant, they retarded for a time the general progress of improvement. The liberality, however, of the employers, in establishing schools at every colliery, is daily effecting a change; and with the advent of another generation the traces of degradation will probably disappear, and there is evidence to lead to a hope that the miner will come to occupy a much-improved position in society."

Most of the population of Inkerman had migrated from Ireland, some being forced out due to the potato blight and resulting famine [1945-52]. They were looking for work and found it initially in the mines, then later in the Oil Works and Brickworks, but also in the Mills.

In his book, *The Irish in Britain* (1894), by John Denvir, he tells us that *"at Linwood, at the Cotton and Paper Mills, and at the coal-pits, you find thriving Irish colonies"*. And in the *Glasgow Observer and Catholic Herald* - Saturday 10 January 1903, we are told *"It is really scandalous that the whole County of Renfrew should only have two branches of the United Irish League within its boundary at present. What is Nitshill and Neilston doing? Both these places had branches, as had Linwood"*.

The *Paisley & Renfrewshire Gazette* reported on the 30th of November 1907 about a large meeting of the *United Irish League* on the previous Tuesday, at Johnstone Town Hall, and that many from Linwood and Houston were in attendance. This included St Conval's first parish priest, Father William Shaw. The meeting was on the subject of continuing the support for *Home-Rule* in Ireland.

And in the Valuation Rolls for the 1920's for Redan Rows there was a 'Reading Room' at No12 which was occupied by the *Ancient Order of Hibernians*.

Evidence of this influx can be seen in many newspaper articles of the period that mention the origins of the people discussed therein, but it can also be seen in the family names of many of the population the, but also in the descendants of those who settled, many of which remain in Linwood town today.

Many of the Irish lived in the mining settlements of Balaclava, Redan, and Inkerman, and their Irish origin surnames can be also seen in the censuses of that period. Indeed, in an article in the *Paisley & Renfrewshire Gazette* on the 06th of February 1875, a Presbytery Missionary called Mr McIndoe, who regularly visited the village and surrounding hamlets, and knew most of the inhabitants, stated that *"the residents of Redan are nearly all Roman Catholics"*. Inkerman was also known to be predominantly Catholic.

The sound of both Northern and Southern Irish accents would have been just as common as Scottish accents in the village and hamlets at during this time. Unfortunately, the collective Irish, Nationalists and Unionists, brought their differences with them, just as they did to the Glasgow shipyards, and this would often manifest itself in drunken fights, and inter-village/hamlet battles based on religious differences.

In the second half of the 19th Century, it was more like *Wild-West* Linwood as there was much violence between the village men, and their assaults on Policemen, usually when drunk, but also there were many cases of wife-beating. During this period there was constant clash between a drunken culture on one side and temperance and abstinence organisations, and the church on the other. Below are three examples of such episodes.

The *Glasgow Herald* reported on the 17th of July 1873 under the heading *"An Irritable Irishman"* of a Linwood miner, named William Love, who *"was yesterday fined 10s 6d, with the option of seven days' imprisonment. William had come to town to witness the Orange display, but as several of the bands of music began to play "The Battle of the Boyne," the miner became excited. He challenged then and there to fight in a single combat any ten Orangemen, but with but one of his hands in use. The police interfered, and locked William up."*

The *Paisley Daily Express* reported on the 23rd of September 1881 under the heading *"A Pugilistic Bandsman"* at the *"Justice of Court this forenoon - before Baileys McGowan and Young – John Berry, described as a labourer residing Redan, was charged with breach of the peace on 10th of Sept., on the public road at various places between the Cart Bridge and the village of Linwood, while in a state of intoxication, by cursing and swearing, and challenging persons to fight. Accused pleaded guilty the charge. It appears that he is a member of the Linwood band. On the day in question, he had been with them, but having "pre'ed the barley bree" he lost control of his head, and fell, damaging his instrument, which was thereupon taken from him. He got riled at this, and began abusing the band, challenging them fight for the Queen. The Fiscal – 'that is not the kind Queen wants" (Laughter). The court then fined him 10s 6d or 10 days."*

The *Paisley & Renfrewshire Gazette* reported on the 18th of August 1877 under the heading *"The Lawlessness of the Miners of the Linwood and Inkerman Districts"*, we were informed that *"No less than eight persons, from the village of Linwood and Inkerman, were charged before the Court with committing breaches of the peace and assaults—the majority of whom were miners. As the several cases were called in succession, the Fiscal pointed out to the Bench the excessive work the police constables had performed in the village, and in one case he introduced the accused by saying "this Linwood again". James Muldoon, labourer, Linwood, pled guilty to committing breach of the peace the 28th ult., or near the public-house, occupied by publican David Robertson, Linwood, between ten and eleven o'clock at night, challenging several persons to fight, and cursing and swearing in a dreadful manner, and by threatening what would do to Mr. Robertson if he would not supply him with drink. The Court asked accused what had to say to the charge. The only palliation Muldoon could plead was the drink, which he stated he bad got too much of, and which was too strong. He was fined 15s, or suffer imprisonment for seven days."*

People may wonder why this period was so violet and disturbing, and for good reason. However, I think the main reason was due to the aforementioned religious differences between the Irish Catholic incomers clashing with native Scottish Protestants, and their incoming Northern Irish counterparts.

In strong contrast to the second half of the 19th Century, Linwood became known as a quiet and sleepy little village again in the early decades of the 20th Century, as it had been since its creation up until this point. The opening of the Good Templars Lodge [temperance organisation] in 1902 would have helped with this transition. The reason for the change I can only suggest was because the previous generation with their cultural and religious differences had largely died off by now, and the new generation were much less bitter, had learned to live together, and just wanted to get on with their lives. But also, because the previous industries of mining and cotton spinning had become defunct and the new industries of engineering and the paper making had succeeded them, and this gave people a new outlook.

In his retiral speech on the 21st of October 1926, the Rev. J. A. Abernethy said: *"Although in a manner Linwood was considered warlike, it was not a fighting parish. The minister and congregation had been very much united, and his people had circled round him more and more. Although they had a great population of Roman Catholics in the parish, the Protestants and they were very kindly to each other, and got on well together. There was no division in the social life, so he felt he was not only leaving home, but a great circle of friends in his old parish."*

Having been Minister for Linwood Parish Church since 1880, the Rev. J. A. Abernethy would have experienced Linwood village move on from the heights of its wild uncontrolled days of the late 19th Century, and its return to a more serene society in the early 1900's.

Moving on to the 1940's, Linwoodonian Sadie Brown recollects the drinking culture thus: *"I remember Saturday nights at closing time at the corner of Hart Street and Bridge Street; the mothers with their weans and babies wrapped in their shawls, waiting for the pubs to spill and it was the highlight and gossip of the week, who's man was the drunkest, and who was fighting with whom."* And subsequently, the output of these skirmishes would be the *"Talk of the Co-op van all week"*.

By 1963 Linwood was to change culturally forever with another influx of outsiders, this time an invasion emanating from Glasgow. The in-situ villagers soon became diluted in the vast swathes of Glaswegians, mostly young couples with young families, and with many children still to come.

For the most part Villagers and incoming Glaswegians got on well, although occasionally there were differences. Linwood's Moyra Chadwick's mother had resented the incomers and she told of change in terms of some locals not trusting incomers, in that the *"Coop shop staff started to insist that shoppers had to be accompanied to look at the clothes" section upstairs, when before you could go alone."*

Those coming in from 1963 until 1972 were housed in new estates, or schemes, and those of Scottish ancestry would sometimes refer to the old village as *'The Vatican City'* due to the higher than usual [for Scotland] Catholic population of Irish ancestry.

With increased population came demand for entertainment and so social clubs were fashioned from buildings of other previous uses, and new ones built. Of course, with it being Scotland, these clubs were created for the different sides of the religious divide, St Conval's and St Brendan's [Celtic Supporters] Social Clubs on one side, and the Rangers' Supporters Social Club and Masonic Social Club on the other. But in reality, and as time moved one, these clubs were largely used by persons that kicked with either foot.

And kids being kids, they played together on the streets and grassy areas within the schemes, and only started to 'see' and 'act-out' their supposed differences as they got into high school.

The new Linwood was brand spanking new in every way; the houses were new, the shopping centre and the schools were new, the streets were clean, playgrounds and street furniture intact and undamaged. However, because the vast majority of incomers came from Glasgow, they brought with them the tenement sense of community, where you could leave your door unlocked, borrow a cup of sugar, and you knew everyone. And this is the way it was for that generation, but by the next generation, and into the 1990's, and right up until today, sadly that sense of community has mostly disappeared.

Many neighbours no longer talk to each other; in-fact they built tall fences between each-others gardens, when they used to have low fences and hedges, natter away to each other over them, and weans would play in each-others gardens.

Most of the Social Clubs and Pubs from the boom days of the 1960's/1970's, have now closed down, as people habits and priorities changed, mainly due to closure of the Car Plant and many families becoming home owners.

People no longer work together in large groups as they did with the bigger employers in the area, and have to commute to work out-of-town and work alongside people from other towns and cities, therefore the previous local sense of comradery is no longer there, i.e., previously it was a case of 'those who work together, drink and socialise together'. And thus, community breaks down, and people hole-up in their bought houses, and stay in at the weekend with a *curry-for-two* from a supermarket.

The Battle of Linwood Bridge

In his excellent journal [RLHF Journal Vol. 6 (1994)] account of *'The Battle of Linwood Bridge'*, author *Brian S. Skillen* gives a great and detailed account of the events of that day on the 12th of July 1859, at the 'Linwood Bridge', which spans the river Black Cart. Therefore, I won't go into great detail here, but rather concentrate of the ongoing cultural differences.

The migration of Northern Irish workers to the mining and textiles industries of the Paisley district introduced many of the problems experienced in religious differences. It seems there was a general division of labour and religion, with Roman Catholics in labouring and in mining, whereas Protestant folk were principally in textiles. However, that division was not always consistent in all cases, and some of the Oversmen (Foremen) in Linwood's ironstone mines were of Irish Protestant stock, many coming from North Ayrshire.

On Tuesday the 12th of July 1859, a little after 6 o'clock, a party of Orangemen, numbering upwards of a hundred, mustered near the cross on decorated with orange sashes, and other party emblems. At half-past six precisely they marched in procession westward along High Street, Wellmeadow Street, etc., with a band of music at their head, and carrying six or seven orange flags. The marchers were well armed and so were likely expecting trouble.

The first skirmish occurred at Millarston. Roman Catholics were the first to resort to actual violence, and the first to flee, which wasn't surprising for the heavily armed Orangemen had beaten off the attack, and the miners had fled bloodied from sword cuts and bludgeons.

The Orange march continued to Johnstone, where they continued on their way toward the mining area about Quarrelton and Corseford, then made its way to Millikenpark, where it turned at the railway station and made its way to Deafhillock Toll [near Brookfield], arriving there about 1.00pm. The Linwood Orangemen left the main march at that point and headed for their village. The Paisley and Johnstone Lodges proceeded for the West [Linwood] Toll, where they intended to go their separate ways. However, as the Orange marchers approached Linwood Bridge, they found their way blocked by a group of angry mine workers. The Miners now numbered some 300 and seeing this the Orangemen scarpered to seek safety of Linwood village. After rallying, it was decided that they would once again try for the bridge and the battle began. Hand-to-hand fighting with mining tools, bludgeons, and knives caused terrible injuries. News of the battle spread quickly and as a result a mob turned up to watch the fight. The fight is reported to have lasted at least 45 minutes, and once the battle was over the process of attending to the injured began and a total of seven Doctors arrived from Paisley and Johnstone.

There were many injured on both sides. Some had been stabbed and slashed, and one man shot in the face with slugs, but most had been badly beaten. However, one fatality had occurred. He was Patrick Rush, a 67-year-old Roman Catholic worker from Paisley, a besom [broom] maker, who had not taken part in the battle, but had been caught by some of the mob and kicked and stabbed to death, as he tried to get clear of the site of the battle. His body was found on the road a considerable distance from Linwood Bridge, pointing to his misfortune in being in the wrong place at the wrong time.

The news of Patrick Rush's death sparked off a strike by the Roman Catholic miners in the Linwood area, they claiming sectarianism, but it turns out that he could have been the victim of either side given the confusion of the affray. His family later said that he wasn't meant to be there, having left home in Paisley at 12pm.

It came to light that the well-armed Orangemen had been helped by the police, who were in some cases on duty and in others having been part of the march, even in uniform, who arrested participants from both sides, and who were then committed for trial.

At the trial three months later, the Advocate Depute, having addressed the jury for the Crown, Mr M'Laren for Mr M'Graw, and Mr Thomson for Brannan, the jury retired, and returned verdict of guilty libelled against M'Graw, at guilty of mobbing and rioting again Brannan, the assault not proven, M'Graw was sentenced to six months', and Brannan four months' imprisonment. The miners, Francis Pinkerton, James Anderson, David Bulloch, James Bulloch, Archibald Anderson, John Pirie and John Barr, were accused of assaulting Hugh Cowan, Peter Cowan, Joseph Elliot and Peter Lawson to their severe injury. These seven miners from Inkerman were heavily fined, with option of jail, for assault. No one was convicted of the killing of Patrick Rush. The affair then faded from the headlines, but Linwood at this time remained a manifestation of religion's ability to destroy working class unity by encouraging sectarian disorder.

Fearing reprisals, the authorities drafting in 150 Royal Sussex Militia from Glasgow to barracks in Paisley 16th of July 1859, to keep the peace.

Four days after the affray, the *Glasgow Herald* reported on the 16th of July on the *"Unsettled State of The Village of Linwood"*, thus:

"Since the affray on Tuesday at the village of Linwood, the whole neighbourhood has been in a state of excitement. The Catholic party vow the direst revenge upon their opponents for the murder of the unfortunate man Patrick Rush, and, on Thursday evening, a feeling was abroad that they would put their threats into execution by attacking the houses of the Orangemen. A strong force of the latter was mustered in Linwood on that evening, and about a hundred of them, armed with fire-arms and other lethal weapons, after parading about, marched from the Redan mining village in the district, through Linwood, till they reached Cartbridge, the scene of the affray. Fortunately, they met with no opposition, or a serious encounter would have taken place. The apathy of the County authorities is a source of wonder and surprise to all. If such demonstrations are allowed to continue, much more fatal consequences than have yet occurred will follow."

On the 23rd of July 1959 the *Glasgow Free Press* reported that a reward had been issued *"for such information, given within one month, as may lead to the apprehension and conviction of the ringleaders in the recent riot at Linwood. A Paisley billsticker, who was employed to post the notices in Linwood, Inkerman and other villages, was rather dubious about the safety of his mission before he set out."*

Some four years later, the *Glasgow Morning Journal* reported on the 10th of December 1863, of a courts case three men, Wm. M'Glachlan, drawer, Patrick M'Glachlan, do., and Edward M'Kinstray, miner, *"all residing in Linwood, were charged with creating a breach of the peace on the previous Saturday evening, by violent and disorderly conduct the streets of the village, threatening to cut and wound, and loud and violent swearing, whereby a crowd was collected to the endangering the public peace. The prisoners all pled guilty, and were fined - one 20s, and the other two in 10s each. An ill-feeling is known to exist between number of the Ribbonmen and Orangemen of the village, and it is supposed the origin of the brawl was a desire on the part of the accused to give some of the latter class a beating."*

Environment & Exploration
Situation

In the 1960's/70's, when the 'Car Plant' incomers generation were growing up in Linwood, we were surrounded by interesting places to go exploring. We were surrounded by fields, forests, farms, rivers and swamps. These places were the Milliken Estate and Brookfield village near Kilbarchan, the Craigends Estate (the 'Manor') at Houston, Moss Woods and 'Red Rocks', and the River Black Cart area between Linwood and Johnstone. Paisley was the big town a bus ride away, and Linwoodonians would travel there to the swimming baths, to the museum, the cinema, but mainly for shopping. Johnstone was a half hour walk away for extra shopping options, the swimming baths and to access their railway station. And there was also the 'Clipper' express bus to take us quickly along the M8 to Glasgow Anderson Bus Station, to a much bigger world.

The Manor Playground

In this section I will sometimes say 'is' or 'was'; this is because some things discussed still exist, while some others no longer do.

The most popular place to go was the 'Manor', which was the old derelict Craigends Estate about 1 mile west of Linwood. The centre point was the 'castle' [Manor house], which lay in ruins. It had an 80m long tunnel running across the back of it, which we dared each other to walk through with our lit 'birthday cake' candles we had purchased out the Clippens road 'paper shop' as we set out on out adventures. There were also the remnants of a wine cellar from which you could still smell the red wine, if my adult memory retrospectively serves me well. For a few years a Kestrel nested high up in the façade and many an *eejit* would scale its heights to get to the nest, buy standing on rusty old masonry nails sticking out from the stonework, and would also try to get to the magnificently sculptured stone lion atop the building.

Behind the 'castle' was a dried-up concrete lined ornamental fish pond and tennis courts overgrown with weeds. And a short walk away was a walled garden which contained an orchard and rows of ruined greenhouses with broken windows and frames, but with plant pots still in their original positions. The surrounding approx. 7m wall had holes in it exposing its cavity, and it is here where a multitude of Jackdaws nested in the springtime.

The front of the 'castle' faced the river Gryfe about 100m down a two-tier hill away, in the middle of which was a water well, which is probably still there in the undergrowth. And on the right at the banks of the river was the 'Dr Who' tree, which is an ancient Yew tree which is still there and has environmental protection. Over the many years of its life, the branches of this unique tree had drooped to ground and taken root to grow into new individual trees in an array around the original old trunk. The result is the branches of this evergreen tree cross-over one another, making it fantastic for kids to be able to swing from tree-to-tree like *Tarzan*, and that is exactly what we did. Great fun.

At the entrance to the estate was an ornate arched gateway and a derelict keepers lodge, with very tall chestnut trees on both sides of the road to the Manor House. These trees were plundered for their chestnuts every autumn by boys to plays *chessies* in the playgrounds of their schools. A little farther up the road branched off to the left, and around 120m along the road were situated the stables, on the banks of the *Locher Water*. These buildings, surrounding a small courtyard, were also derelict. Strangely, the walls inside were decorated with a kind of fresco of nude people; it is not clear whether they were there when the estate was operational, or whether they were added by a *Banksy* of that period; say in the late 1960's.

At the rear of the estate was a small row of cottages, which we were scared to go near as we thought it was haunted. My own 'proof' of that was the door of the first cottage had the horns of Ram, or something such like, mounted on the front. However, as I found out in later years, this was the *Home Farm* of the estate owners, the Cunninghames', there for the state staff, to provide food for them.

And at the back of estate, just over the bridge over the Gryfe, and 80m to right, is 'The Rocks'. This place is a deep-water ravine which the river *Gryfe* rushed through, at the end of which is a pool area, followed by rapids flowing down by the nearby 'Dr Who' tree. The rocky plateau about 4m above the river water was the ideal stance for leaping off into the depths of the *Gryfe*. The water was freezing, but you don't really notice this when you're young, and just get on with the frivolity. Gangs of children from Linwood would have a day-out in

Manor and swimming would often play a part in their day. Rolls on Spam would be made-up and taken on these expeditions to keep up the sustenance of the *weans*. About a mile and a half down-stream was another swimming venue called the Mud-Cliffs, aka Clay-Pits, which was also popular. And we also fished the Gryfe for *Brown Trout* and *Grayling*. This river was relatively clean, but would on occasion be polluted by industry upstream in Bridge of Weir, resulting in multitudes of dead trout floating upside down and flowing downstream to the Clyde.

The Manor was made up of wooded areas and a couple of fields with dairy cows munching the cud. Many of the trees were tall pines and spruces, and some of them still exist there today, although most has been replaced by housing estates. It was great for bird-nesting, climbing trees, exploring and lighting fires – to make tea in a tin can, but not for practising arson.

To sum up, the Manor was the playground of Linwood's *weans*. To us it was *Narnia and Nirvana* rolled into one.

Moss Woods

Split into two main areas by the Moss Road, Moss Woods is dense woodland made-up of naturally growing birch and pine trees sections, and farmed fir trees sections. On the outskirts of the latter is Moss Cottage, which has been there since the 19th Century and was for many years occupied by Gamekeepers of the estate. Many from Linwood would come to go bird-nesting in an environment which was particularly good for Woodpeckers, Treecreepers and various birds of prey. It also had a great variety of flora, butterflies and bees. Much of the forest floor is *'floating'*, due to the high water-table in the area that was once under the Clyde Estuary. I can remember jumping up and down on the ground as a youngster and watching the ground reverberate like a water-bed.

On the east side Moss Woods, near the M8 motorway, was the 'Red Rocks', which was the remnants of old Victorian mineral works. It was like a moonscape of red coloured rocks sitting in pools of shallow water. It was of interest to Linwood kids because of its *other world* look and because frogs, frogspawn, tadpoles and newts could be found there extensively. Some would be captured and taken home, such is the way of fascinated kids.

Adjacent to the woods on the Linwood side is a no-longer used Landfill area, which was known as *Moss Dump* in years gone by when it was used to dump general household waste and by the nearby Incinerator to dispose of the ashes from their burnings. In the 1970's in particular, some Linwood people would scavenge what they could from there, i.e., wheels from old prams to make bogies, and bicycle frames and wheels to make up hybrid bikes. The landfill area is today grassed over and the subject of what its contents are remain controversial.

The River Cart

The stretch of the river than runs by the south-east side of Linwood can be described part slow moving on the upstream side, and fast flowing on the downstream side. This is because of the damn and weir situated just behind the Kintyre Avenue estate. A *Lade* also branches off here and runs roughly parallel to the river down to the village, where it once fed the water supply to the mills.

Some swam here in the damn/weir area, but most wouldn't as it was *manky*. You were liable to catch some disease or rip yourself on an old *Galbraith's* shopping trolley. Some built rafts out of railway sleepers or old oil drums tied together with rope, then they would *punt* their way up and down the upper river section pretending to be *Tom Sawyer* or *Huckleberry Fin*.

The angling was good though, with Pike, Perch, Roach and some Brown Trout in residence. There were no Salmon and Sea Trout – they came several years later when new Environmental Laws were implemented and so the river was cleaned up, encouraging these fish to migrate upstream. And then there was the Legend of *'Big Hector'* the Pike, back in that 1960's to 1980's period. He, or she, roamed the Cart and terrorised Perch, Roach, and Anglers alike. There was a story going around that he once swallowed some ones wee *Jack Russel* dog, and many claims that he had been caught, but it was never proved. Perhaps 'Big Hector' is still around, as female Pike live for many years.

As previously mentioned, the river Black Cart was polluted, mainly due to sewerage and effluents from industry being emitted upstream at Johnstone town. This had been the way since the first Industrial Revolution. Linwood's own emissions were discharged of downstream at mills, and by 1970 had its own sewerage works at the start of Middleton Road.

An example of the pollution was reported in the *Paisley & Renfrewshire Gazette* with the heading *'The State of the Cart'*, on the 11th of May 1907. Its article read: - *"The attention of the Council was drawn to the fact that the residenters at Linwood were complaining of the obnoxious and offensive condition of the river Cart, caused by the discharge into it of the sewage of the burgh of Johnstone. The river was so polluted as to constitute a serious menace to the public health, and fears were expressed that in the summer months it might give rise to an epidemic."*

Brookfield

Brookfield is a small village about ¾ of a mile from East Fulton estate in Linwood and consists of only a few streets. It's was, and perhaps still is, a very middle-class area and used to have sign up at its entrance stating that it was a private road for residents only. So, there should be no surprise that we Linwood urchins were not welcomed there by most of the inhabitants, and we were often chased out. Never-the-less, we went there; mainly for stealing apples, pears and plums out of their gardens, but sometimes by knocking on their doors and asking *"any windfalls Misses/Mister?"*.

The other reason we would walk to near Brookfield village was to use the *Houston and Crosslee* railway station on its outskirts. It was here that we could get the train to Paisley Canal and Glasgow Central Stations, to the latter for many football games at *Hampden*.

The Milliken Estate

Situated between just outside Linwood between the Deafhillock Roundabout and Kilbarchan Quarry, this estate was known by different names with Linwood folks. *Lang's* estate was one, the *Canyon* was another (probably due to the quarry). The owners of the estate lived in a big 'white house' with a walled garden probably an old orchard, nearby. The grounds had wooded areas, one with an ornamental fish pond, and fields and stables. There was also a small trout pond with a burn running into and out of it. In one of the adjacent fields stood, and still does, the ancient *Tower of Milliken*, which was a doocot to keep pigeons destined for the Millikens' winter larder.

Linwood Public Park

Linwood Public Park opened formally to the public on the 13th of September 1930, as reported in the Paisley and Renfrewshire Gazette, although football was played there since the 19th Century. Later, in 1971 the new village bypass 'Perimeter Road' would cut about a third of its area away. Linclive Farm is shown at the top of the photo to the right of Candren Road.

View from the North-East looking at Public Park, with football pitches, tree-lined river Black Cart, gardening allotments – gifted by Captain Spiers in 1886, the road into Linwood village over the old Cart bridge, Holm Terrace tenement at start of Bridge Street, with Holm Pit bing behind it. The St Conval's presbytery can also be seen through the trees on the bottom left

In our *Auld Linwood Town and Surrounds* Facebook Group, I asked the following question of our members – *"If you could select a long-gone Aspect of Linwood to bring back, what would that be?"* The results of the top three answers were: The Manor = 43%; Grahams Buses = 18%; The Railway = 10%. It is clear therefore, that the wonderful playground we called 'the manor', is the easily the most missed as it brings back to us so many great memories of playing, adventure, and of freedom. We can also see that effective and reliable transport is greatly missed. I think it's reasonable to conclude that both these services met their demise due to the closing of the car factory in 1981 - the trains going in 1983, then the buses in 1990.

Health
Johnstone Infectious Diseases Hospital

This hospital was situated just outside Linwood on the Johnstone side of the Railway line border, and was built in 1887 originally as the Johnstone Infectious Diseases (I.D.) Hospital, at a cost of £2,794 4s 10d. In 1911 an annex hospital was built nearby at what would later become Muirhead Drive in 1963, and was known locally at the 'Tin Hospital' due to the roofs being constructed of corrugated tin. Both were known as 'Fever', 'Combination' and 'Isolation' hospitals at various times over the years. They were both also used to treat soldiers during WW2.

The I.D. hospital then cared for geriatric patients well into the 20th century, then was demolished and replaced with a new housing estate in 2022.

The 'Tin Hospital' was used to house the homeless and travelling workers in the 1950's and in the 1960's part of it for community groups such as the Scouts Cubs and for Film Shows. In the early 1970's it was demolished and a disabled school was built there, which in 2005 would be replaced with a new housing estate.

Johnstone I.D. Hospital – circa 1963. Built in 1887. Muirhead House shown on right-hand side of photo.

West Renfrewshire Combination [or Tin] Hospital at Muirhead Drive and brand new Cowal Drive – circa 1963.

A Rare Condition

A very rare and strange condition was reported in the *Carlisle Journal* on Saturday the 16th of June 1838, upon the death of Linwood woman Margaret Barr aged just 23. As follows.

"She was perhaps the most remarkable specimen of the human form in miniature in the Kingdom. She stood thirty inches in height, (and, with the exception of her head, which was rather large) her frame was not out of proportion. No reason could be assigned for her stinted growth. Her mind had the imbecility of a weakly child of two years, and in her last illness, she had the feeble appearance of extreme old age."

On checking the above symptoms, it could be that Margaret was suffering from a 'Progeria', also known as *Hutchinson-Gilford Progeria Syndrome*.

Cholera

On Monday the 29th of January 1849, the *Glasgow Herald* gave details of a Cholera Epidemic of *"extreme virulence"* that had spread over the past few weeks in the west of Scotland. For the section on Kilbarchan Parish its report read as follows.

"Thursday Evening - It is now about three weeks since the cholera made its appearance in this quarter, and when we consider the bounds of the parish and the extent of the population, the consequent mortality has not been so fatal here as it has been in many other places. The report from the parish surgeon (who is very active

and severely toiled) is 20 cases, 16 deaths, and 4 in recoveries. Ten of the sufferers. now dead, resided in this village, 5 in the village of Linwood, and 1 in the country."

Nearly two months later, on the 21st of March 1849, the *Glasgow Chronicle* reported on a presentation held in Linwood by the Kilbarchan Board of Health, to Mr. Mathews, medical student. The Chairman presented Mr. Mathews with a silver lancet-case of beautiful workmanship, bearing the following inscription: — " *Presented to Mr. John Mathews by the Kilbarchan Board of Health, in token of their esteem for his successful treatment of cholera in the village of Linwood —Feb., 1849."*

Typhus

For several years in the mid-19th century the deadly disease Typhus was also prevalent in Linwood, at the same time as Cholera. This disease is spread by bacteria spreading to humans via fleas, lice, and mites, so informs us as to the living conditions at the time.

The victims were mainly workers in Linwood's cotton mills, and the shale, coal and ironstone mines. But not even men of God were immune from the terrible afflictions which caused fatal vomiting, diarrhoea, purple rashes, headaches and fever. Father William Paterson of St Margaret's Church, Johnstone, died of typhus in 1853, aged just 29, after catching the disease during a pastoral visit to a family in Linwood. His predecessor, Father John Bremner, also succumbed to typhus in 1848.

The typhus and cholera victims were buried in mass grave at the corner of Fulwood Avenue and Moss Road, where Mosswood Care Home is today. This mound became known as 'Daisy Hill' and was said by locals to be haunted by the ghosts of plague victims, weeping and wailing and wrapped from head to foot in funeral shrouds. Perhaps it was the patrons of the Golden Pheasant Hotel bar, built there in 1967, that saw these ghosts when departing at throwing out time?

Smallpox

It was reported in the *Glasgow Herald* on the 21st of December 1874 that there were thirteen cases of Smallpox being treated in the Paisley hospitals. The article pointed out that two of these cases had been admitted from Linwood, but that Linwood had largely managed to avoid the disease during past eighteen month when it had been prevalent.

Typhoid

Another deadly disease struck Linwood in 1879, as reported in the *Paisley & Renfrewshire Gazette* on the 20th of December. It was Typhoid, which is spread by sewage contamination of food or water, or through person-to-person contact.

"A very sad case has occurred at Linwood. Mr. James M'Glin, his wife, and three children, were attacked with typhoid fever, and also lodger who was in the house. There were in all nine persons living in single apartment when the malady broke out. The lodger became convalescent, the case the husband and wife became precarious. The parochial authorities visited the house on several occasions, and ultimately resolved to remove the husband, wife, and two of the children were taken to Cowglen Hospital, about seven miles from Linwood. The husband, however, died when taken out of bed. The mother, with the two children who were also suffering from typhoid, were placed in the van; the mother having also taken the infant who was not affected with the disease. The mother only survived till Monday, when she also died, leaving six children."

Again, this tells us much about the living conditions at the time, a family having had to take in a lodger, probably due to poverty, but living cheek-by-jowl unfortunately aided the spread of the disease.

Scarlet Fever

The North British Daily Mail reported on the 23rd of February 1892, that *"It is understood that due to the prevalence of Scarlet Fever disease in the Linwood in has been it has been considered expedient to close the public school."*

Measles

The case of an epidemic of Measles in Linwood was reported in the *Greenock Telegraph and Clyde Shipping Gazette* on the 09th April 1892, in which Dr Munro (Renfrew County Medical Officer of Health) gave details in his report.

The disease had been circulating for seven weeks since the 07th of January. But wasn't going away. So, by the 17th March it become apparent that the disease was out of hand, and so Dr Munro wired the Clerk the School Board to secure the immediate closure of the Board School, which was at once closed. For the next fortnight the disease, prevailed amongst families whose children had been infected before date of the closure the school. The number of cases declined and within a fortnight the epidemic was practically extinct far as this line of school attendance was concerned.

Dr Munro had also advised the authorities in charge the Catholic school to close; they, however, declined the ground that only three cases had up that date occurred amongst the children. On the 2nd of March, he again wired imperatively pressing for the closure of the school, and the school was then closed. The mischief had, however, been done; the disease had become epidemically prevalent amongst the Catholic school children and in this way was introduced into the village of Blackstoun, which had previously been free from disease.

The epidemic eventually became extinct, but in the previous six weeks there had occurred 143 cases in the village Linwood, 53 in Clippens, 10 in Blackstoun, and there had been six deaths. The lesson to be learnt from this sad eventful history that whenever measles makes its appearance amongst children attending a village school the school would be closed at once.

Mental Health

In 1866, it was reported in the Renfrewshire Independent on the 30th of June that the Kilbarchan Parochial Board had carried-out their half-yearly meeting in which they discussed the source of the lunatic pauperism of the mining and manufacturing districts of Linwood. £200 had already been paid towards the care of the lunatic paupers and it was *"mentioned that out of 40 persons chargeable to the Board in Linwood, 35 were natives of the Green Isle"*. A board member's report had advocated *"a poorhouse for the parish pensioners, as being most conducive to their health and wellbeing"*, but this was dismissed as the board deemed that there already be *"ample poorhouse accommodation in Paisley and Greenock"*.

The question may be asked as to why there was such a high rate of Irish nationals being lunatic paupers in Linwood. Perhaps it could have been knock-on effect from poor health emanating from the Irish Potato Famine just twelve years before, when many Irish came to Linwood and surrounding villages for work in the mines and manufacturing industries.

Sanitation and Hygiene

The sanitary conditions and hygienic habits of some Linwoodonians in the 19th and early 20th Centuries left nothing to be desired, and often led to the spread of disease and fever.

The *Glasgow Herald* reported on the 27 of April 1872 that Kilbarchan Parochial Board were informed of a fever spreading *"something like an epidemic form"* in an area of the village known as the 'Black Land'. The Board then instructed the Sanitary Inspector and Medical Officer to arrange the removal of the reluctant patents to the infirmary of the infected houses for the purpose of *"cleaning and fumigation"* to *"take the most effectual means in their power to have these objects carried out"*.

The *Paisley & Renfrewshire Gazette* reported on the 01st of December 1900 about a 'cleaning duties of tenants' case heard in the Paisley Sheriff Court the previous Monday against three men residing in four cottages known as Barrowman's Pit Houses, or cottages (where the T-junction of Melrose Avenue is today). They were *"charged with an infringement of Section 31 of the Public Health (Scotland) Act, 1801, in so far as the privies and the approaches thereto connected with the cottages were, in the opinion of the Sanitary Inspector, in such a state as to be a nuisance for want of proper cleansing. The respondents pleaded not guilty; but after proof the Sheriff found were fined each in 5s each."*

The *Dundee Evening Telegraph* reported on the 31st of August 1921 about an 'Ejectment Decree' against a tenant due to the unsanitary conditions of the house she lived in. She was the wife of a Pig Breeder and had continued to occupy a house after it had been uncertified fit for habitation due to not having a water supply and sanitary conveyance. The lady told the court that *"if they put her out, she'd have to go into the fields as she could get no house, and hadn't had a doctor in years"*. She was duly fined £1 and £1 5s expenses.

Disease Prevention

With a permanent water supply being piped into Linwood from Paisley from 1872 it was reported that this was helping with the prevention of the spread of disease and fever symptoms. The *Glasgow Herald* reported on the 01st of June 1872 that *"From the report of a sub-committee, appointed at a former meeting, it appeared that, owing to the epidemic form in which fever had appeared in Linwood, it had been found necessary to employ a person to attend to the removal of fever patients, and to superintend the disinfecting and cleansing of the houses, bed and body clothing, &c. The measures adopted have been very successful, for apparently the spread of the disease has been checked, no new case having occurred during the past week."* This improvement would permanently help prevent the spread of such diseases as cholera, diarrhoea, typhoid, hepatitis, gastroenteritis, scabies, and worm infections

Suicides

Over the history of Linwood there have been many suicides, and attempted suicides, most of which were committed in the Lade and the River Black Cart. One example of special note occurred in April 1899, thus: whilst looking for the body of a missing person in the River Black Cart, police found the body of Mr James Mitchell, Headmaster of Linwood Public School, in the Lade near the Paper Mill. Mr Mitchell, who was 50 years of age, had been depressed for some time and only the previous week a temporary teacher was appointed to discharge his duties until his recovery.

Infanticides

It's a mystery why some women, thankfully a miniscule percentage, kill their babies. It may due to mental health issues brought on by severe circumstances, such as babies being born out of wedlock, which in the 19th and early 20th Centuries was extremely unacceptable, as the woman/girl could be ostracised from society, and lose her job, and thus face a dire future for her and her baby. Below are three examples of infanticides committed in Linwood.

In October 1870, Mary McArthur, delivered a baby in the house of Alexander Gardener, Engineer and Spirit Dealer (Public House Owner), in Linwood village. Shortly afterwards she walked 90 yards to the Mill Lade and threw the child into the water, which was two feet in depth, and the child drowned. Sergeant Macrae, after returning to Linwood from Paisley on Monday, was put in possession of information which led him to think that the mother of the child was a married woman, who was working as domestic servant to Mr Gardner, spirit merchant, Linwood. She had, however, left her situation on that day, and said that she was going to Partick to see a brother. Sergeant Macrae determined then to return to Paisley to consult the county police authorities there, when he accidentally met the woman on the road near Linclive Farm, and apprehended her. She is said to have been married seven years ago, but her husband shortly afterwards left her and went to America. She is about 30 years of age, and her name is Mary M'Arthur, a native of Islay. In late December that same year she was found guilty of culpable homicide and sentenced to five years penal servitude.

Just one month later, in November 1870, on a Sunday morning, Mrs Carney of Redan Rows in Linwood village was in the act of taking some water from the Mill lade which runs through the village, when she discovered the dead body of a newly born infant lying close to the bank. The body was quite naked and it had the appearance of having only been in the water a short time. Police were informed and the body removed. A *post mortem* examination of the body of the child was made by the pathologist who found that the child had been born alive and afterwards drowned.

In May 1908, a man-servant from a farm two miles north-west of Linwood was shocked to discover the dead body of a child in a garden, which was male and appeared to be newly born. A maid-servant, originally from Lesmahagow, was believed to be the mother of the child, and she was promptly taken away to an 'institution' for medical attention. Police were investigating the distressing affair.

Accidents

Accidents have occurred in Linwood over the years, just as in any village or town. Many of these were drowning's were in the Mill Lade and the River Cart due to people stumbling and falling-in, due to swimming sessions going wrong, and due to alcohol intoxication. Other accidents occurred in the farms, mines and the factories.

Some of the more tragic and notable accidents are given below.

On the 12th of February 1859, the *Paisley Herald and Renfrewshire Advertiser* reported on a case of a boy who was scalded to death. The accident occurred *"in the neighbourhood of the Old Candren Pit, between Inkermann and Linwood. Some persons were pumping the water from a boiler into a ditch, (a process performed once a-week or so), when a boy, between 5 and 6 years of age, named John Gall, son of the Pitheadman, of the same name, stumbled accidentally into the ditch, and the water being nearly boiling hot, he was so fearfully scalded, that he died hours afterwards, in the utmost agony. It was nearly dark when the poor boy missed his footing, and fell into the water. He was extricated as speedily possible; and Dr Taylor was sent for immediately, but the scalding was too severe permit of recovery."*

On the 05th of July 1875 the *Dundee Courier* reported sad and tragic case of a little girl accidently shot by her older brother. *"At Redan, Linwood, on Tuesday night, melancholy affair occurred which threw a gloom over the neighbourhood. A man named Beith, who is connected with Green Farm, had taken home loaded gun with the intention of shooting crows next day on the farm. He unfortunately placed it within the reach of his children. During the absence of the parents, a lad about 10 years of age, took down the gun, and while handling it, it was accidentally discharged. The contents lodged in the head of his little sister, five years old, and shattered her skull to pieces. Medical assistance was speedily procured, but the child died almost immediately after the shot had been fired."*

In 1889, one man, a native of Ireland, overbalanced when leaning out of his one-storey dwelling house in Linwood village, and died.

One accident that had a big effect on the folks of Linwood village was reported in the *Central Somerset Gazette* on the - Saturday 05th of February, 1898. A shocking burning accident at a house resulting in the death of two children and their mother. The house (where the T-Junction of Melrose Avenue is today) was situated about 200 yards off the Johnstone and Linwood [Bridge of Weir] Road, just opposite the Clippens Works, and about a quarter of a mile from Linwood village. It was a one-storey building of a cluster being locally known as "Barrowman's Row" and 'Barrowman Cottages", of which there were four. It appears that a man named John

Leitch, a barrowman, was on the previous Tuesday boiling tar to be used in mending the roof of the hen-house, and in lifting the pot off the fire he tripped and the boiling liquid fell about his wife, his three children, and a lodger named James Bingley. The inmates were for a time confined to the burning room, and were all badly burned before they were enabled to get out. The six persons were removed to the hospital at Elderslie, and there two of the children, James, aged six years, and Lizzie, aged eight years, died together with Mrs. Leitch.

Mr James Bingley lay in Johnstone Cottage hospital for nearly two years due to his injuries and was released in December 1899 after undergoing the amputation of an arm and a foot. It was thought that by these operations that his life would be prolonged, but, unfortunately, his health was so severely shattered that, after lingering in much rain and suffering, he passed away on the 26th of May 1900. Mr. Bingley, a Timekeeper at R & W Watson's Papermill, was a man who was well known in the locality. He took an active interest in the social well-being of the village, especially in temperance work amongst the young, and also in the Free Gardeners.

An 8-foot ionic (Celtic) cross grey-granite stone was soon erected at Kilbarchan New Cemetery. It remains there today and has the following inscription: - *"Erected by public subscription to the memory of James Bingley, who died at Linwood on 26th May, 1900, aged 44 years, from injuries received at the Barrowman's burning disaster in his heroic efforts to save the lives of those endangered. Truly he was a man"*. But what memorial is there to the family that also perished?

Doctor Practices in Linwood

The first record of any doctor being based in Linwood is from 1928 when a Dr McKellar practiced there. Before this the people of Linwood consulted with doctors mainly from Johnstone, and sometimes from Paisley

The first doctors practice that anyone can remember of, is the one that was located in a 'house' building at the corner of Bridge of Weir and South Drive from the 1940's, which still stands today, and at which Dr Kinloch, Dr Houston and Dr McCusker practiced at various times.

The next practice was just around the corner in a 2-storey tenement Greenhill Terrace on Bridge Street, from around the 1950's to mid-1960's, and at which Dr Houston, Dr Stewart and Dr McCusker practiced at various times.

St Conval's Parish Church also had a practice based out of a hut at the entrance of the 'horses park' in the 1950's, which moved in the 1960's to Napier Street. This hut was also used for changing by St Conval's football team. Dr McCusker was also known to have practiced here.

For a brief period of 2 or 3 years in the mid-late 1960's there was a practice situated on the ground floor of the 2-storey tenement called Park Place, which still stands today. Dr McCusker was also known to have practiced here.

These practices ceased and during the late 1960's a temporary practice in a hut on the corner of Bridge Street and south Napier Street, where Dr Malcolm and Dr Cunningham practised until December 1970 when they moved to the new clinic in Ardlamont Square in the new shopping centre.

In December 1970 the Linwood Clinic opened for business, but wasn't formally opened until the 22nd of July 1971, and still going today. There have been many Doctors' working here over the past half century, and so too many to mention, however Dr Malcolm, Dr Cunningham continued their there, and the likes of Dr Todd, Dr Dunlop and Dr Richmond came in later years.

Crime and Punishment

Linwood has had its share of murders over the years, but not too numerous, and in any case, not for discussion here. Apart from thefts, examples of which are given below, most of the crimes were related to those men who were intoxicated with alcohol, especially in the period of the second half of the 19th Century, as discussed in the *Culture* section of this book. There were many cases of violence between miners, wife beatings, and assaults on Policemen.

So below, I discuss the other types of crimes committed in the district of Linwood, and in some cases, from a different angle.

Harsh Sentences for Petty Crimes

In July 1859, at Glasgow Sherriff Court, a male labourer was sent to prison for 30 days for stealing a cart load of heather and a 30 feet long board from Linwood Moss farm, the property of Thomas Speirs, Esquire., of Blackstoun.

In Jan 1862, a woman living at the Balaclava hamlet, was charged before the Sherriff with having stolen a small quantity of coals from the Clippens No. 3 pit, near Linwood, and was subsequently sentenced to 15 days imprisonment as it had come to light, that she had done this on several occasions of late.

Similarly, at the Justice of the Peace Court in Paisley on the August 1875, a ten-year-old boy was sentenced to five years confinement at the Industrial School for stealing a small quantity of coals from a pit in the neighbourhood of the village. The boy's father had stated that he had lost control over him, and in time past he had committed all manner of petty thefts.

In March 1894 two Linwood boys were ordered to receive five stripes (the cane) and three stripes respectively for maliciously breaking four panes of glass in a window of a dwelling-house at Linwood on the 21st of February. A condition was added that should the medical officer certify them to be unfit for such punishment, that they be fined 5s or three days in jail.

In June 1896 a Linwood boy was sent to prison for 7 days at the Justice of the Peace Court for defrauding a woman. It was explained that he had extorted 4s from her by pretending to have repaired a broken cup and lid with Egyptian cement, which had been handed to him for that purpose.

At the Juvenile Court in March 1952 two boys were sentenced for breaking into a house and stealing a biscuit tin containing biscuits, a purse and 8s of money, two sweet ration coupons, 19 tea tokens and a packet of playing cards. One of them, who had a previous record of stealing, was sent to a remand home for three weeks. The other was put on two years' probation.

Stupid and Amusing Crimes

At a trial in July 1872, the Sherriff and the jury were informed about the case of two gamekeepers called Wilson and Cameron, who, it was alleged, assaulted an engineer named Pattison, by throwing him in the river and carrying away a quantity of fish which he had angled. The case went to proof, but the outcome is unknown.

At Paisley Sherriff Court in December 1899, two labourers were sent to prison for 14 days for stealing a hen and two ducks from a hen-house at Barrowman's Cottages, near Linwood.

On the 04th of October 1979, a nightshift employee of *Chrylser* car plant decided to play a prank on his dayshift colleagues. The employee phoned the *Chrysler Social Club* saying there as a bomb about to explode. The Glasgow Sherriff Court heard that there was an almighty panic in the club and pints and nips were scattered as the place emptied in a rush. However, the joke backfired when police traced the call back to his home in Castlemilk and later arrested him. The accused told the judge that he had meant no harm and was just doing it for a dare. The judge fined him £200.

On the 11th of May 1993 there was another bomb hoax in Linwood. This time it was from a disgruntled employee of *Watson and Grange Limited's* Paper Mill. The employee had made a 999 call and told the startled operator *"There's a bomb in the Paper Mill in Linwood"*. Around fifty workers were then quickly evacuated and police search the building, where the company later claimed they had lost between £6,000 and £8,000 in lost production. Police had managed to trace the call back as the quick-thinking operator had not hung up; she was still on the other end when police entered his house. The accused pleaded guilty to the charge and was sentenced to 200 hours of unpaid community work. He told the judge he done it because he hated the backshift and was just looking for a couple of hours off. His employers fired him for his actions.

Late 20th Century Robberies

On Tuesday 30 December 1969, a gang of three robbers attacked a *Clydesdale Bank* branch in Bridge Street, Linwood. The leader of the gang was Howard Wilson, a former police officer who had resigned, disillusioned at his lack of promotion and now in debt. The others were John Sim, a policeman-turned-salesman, and Ian Donaldson, a car mechanic. At precisely 3.15 p.m. the raiders entered the bank. They were unmasked and were armed with a pistol, a dagger, and a knife. They also had with them several pillow-cases, some string, and two suitcases. The manager, Mr. Fleming, was out and Mr. Mackin, the assistant manager, showed all three into the manager's office. Then, without warning, he was thrown aside and the door was closed. Mr. Mackin was about to protest when a pistol was pressed against his temple along with the warning: *"If we have full co-operation no member of the staff will be harmed."* With that, a pillow-case was placed over Mr. Mackin's head and his hands were bound. Seconds later, Mr. Fleming returned. As he entered his office a gun was placed against his neck and he was warned to be silent. Another pillow-case was thrown over his head and his hands were bound.

In the bank at the time, but quite unaware of the situation in the manager's office, were a man and two girls, members of the staff, and a customer, a Mr. Gibb. Suddenly, the raiders emerged from the manager's office and held all four at gun-point. None made a move and patiently submitted to being thrust into the manager's office, where pillow-cases were put over their heads and their wrists were bound.

While this was taking place, local lady Mrs. Margaret Pirie, wheeling her two-year-old son in his pram, knocked on the bank door. One of the raiders opened the door, but the moment she stepped inside she was forced at gunpoint into the manager's office. She was later allowed to bring her son into the bank. The safe was open and all the notes and a large quantity of silver coins were packed into three leather cases. In all, the raiders got away with £14,212.

Shortly after they robbed the bank, a City of Glasgow Police officer, Inspector Andrew Hyslop, spotted them unloading the loot (which amounted to around £14,000) from a car into a flat in Allison Street, Glasgow. Hyslop just happened to be passing and was not yet aware of the robbery but thought the trio were acting suspiciously. When he investigated with some of his colleagues, Wilson pulled out a handgun and shot three officers, all in the head: Hyslop, Acting Detective Constable Angus MacKenzie, and Police Constable Edward Barnett. Another constable, John Sellars, took refuge in the flat's bathroom and radioed for backup. As MacKenzie lay wounded on the floor, Wilson held the gun to his forehead and shot again; he was about to shoot Hyslop again when he was tackled and disarmed by Police Constable John Campbell. MacKenzie died at the scene and Barnett in hospital a few days later, while Hyslop's injuries confined him to a wheelchair for life

On the 04th of November 1991 a bunch of blundering raiders armed with a hand-gun attached and 'robbed' a security man outside *Presto's* food store in Linwood. For when they opened the cash-box they discovered it was empty, because they had been unaware that the money had just been delivered to the shop on Burnbrae Road minutes earlier. No shots were fired and no one was injured, and the getaway car was later found on Candren Road, Ferguslie.

In late June 1992 two masked men held up the *Venture Bar* on Bridge Street in Linwood. Owner George Davidson and five bar staff were herded into a corner before pointing a shotgun into George's stomach and ordering him to hand over the money or they would kill him, which he did, then they ran off.

On 19th of January 1993 a Gunman held up the *Halifax* section of the *Stirling and Mair* Solicitors in Bridge at lunchtime and escaped with £11,000. No shots were fired and no one was hurt, although one female member of staff was badly shaken and had to see here doctor.

In the 1990's, there were two robberies at the *Clippens Inn* pub on Clippens Road. The first was in June 1994 when a business-man was getting into his car out the pub he was held-up at knifepoint and £7,000 was taken from him. The three robbers then made off in a car, which was later found abandoned in Kintyre Avenue. The second was on the 04th of January 1999 when two masked men, one with a gun and one with a knife, robbed the pub of a four-figure sum at 11.30am. The five members of staff and a number of customers were shaken by their ordeal.

On the 10th of January 1996, around 07.50am, just before it was due to open, Linwood's *Capital Foods* shop in Ardlamont Square was held up by robbers who held a gun against the stomach of the shop's deputy manager. The terrified woman was ordered to keep quiet, do what she was told, then forced to open the office safe. Second later, the robbers who were wearing hooded jackets and scarfs over their faces, escaped on foot with over £2,000. No one was hurt and no shots were fired.

In January 1998 a gang of cash machine raiders got away with over £40,000 after cleaning out the 'hole in the wall' machine at the *Bank of Scotland* in Armour Place in Linwood. Apparently, the thieves had gotten into back of the dispenser after breaking through the main door. Bank officials were too embarrassed to talk about it.

As bad as the crimes listed above may have been, by far the biggest crime of all that occurred at Linwood, albeit a moral crime, was Thatcher's closing down of the Car Plant.

Living Conditions

Late 18th and the 19th Century living conditions were very basic and life was tough, not just in Linwood, but all over the country. Many of the homes in Linwood's only two streets were provided by the owners of the mills and many were two or three storey tenements consisting of flats that were small and overcrowded. In 1861, 64% of Scotland's population lived in either a single-end (one room) or room and kitchen (two rooms). Up to 15 people might live in a single end. They would sleep in a bed recess instead of a bedroom. Often people shared a bed and slept top-to-tail. There was no running water, just a communal tap. People shared a standpipe in the street to get water. They used an outdoor toilet called a privy, from which sewage would run into the streets and rubbish was thrown into the street with no-one to collect it. These unhealthy conditions and overcrowding often led to health problems and outbreaks of disease.

The following are two first-hand accounts of the living conditions in Linwood in the middle 20th Century.

John McSporran

Linwood lady Mrs Sarahanne Doyle kindly provided me with copies of hand written notes left by her dear Papa John McSporran (1927-2017). In it he recounts the location and living conditions of his upbringing, as follows.

"I lived in Armour Place, [Bridge Street] Linwood, in a single room facing the back door which had two wash greens and a stone wash house. Within the tenement were nine homes on three levels. There were no bath rooms in any of the houses, water was provided by a single cold tap for a kettle boiled on a gas cooker in a small kitchenette room, [and] for personal washing and boiling vegetables and other foods.

I remember meals being cooked on what was known as the metal gauge which provided all the heating from a coal fire located on one side of the range, the other side included [a] two level oven for keeping food plates warm.

There were two beds in the single room fitted into two spaces which in Scotland is known as "Holes in the Wa" in Scots, i.e., 'Wall'.

I remember we went on a regular basis to my Aunt Mary in Bridge Street for a bath. Lots of people went to family members who had a bath within the homes, this was in the 1930's".

Moyra Chadwyck

Another Linwood lady Mrs Moyra Chadwyck moved from Linwood to Jersey in the 1960, and gives the following account of where she was brought up and the living conditions there in the late 1930's until her departure.

"I was born in Moss Cottage, Moss Toll in 1936. My parents, grandparents and my brothers and sisters - five of them at that time, had already lived there for a few years, but I don't know who lived there before them. There were twelve (one twin died) of us lived my gran, seven brothers and sisters and mum and not forgetting there was a set-in bed in the kitchen where my grandparents slept what you now call your living room. It was always a big happy home with many visitors. My eldest brother Peter must have been fifteen or there about when I was born. Some of us still lived there in dwindling numbers, two of my brothers going off to WWII, until after my dad died in the 1970, and so my mum was there on her own after it being a house full of life, so she sold it to a taxi driver and then moved to Shaw place.

We didn't have any stove for years my mum cooked on the open fire for years; it was in the kitchen the scullery and was only for washing up.

Years later we got a Calor gas cooker as we didn't have electricity until my brother was working and he put all the electric wires in and connected us to electricity grid.

We had a bathroom with a bath but only had cold water so had to light the big boiler in the wash house and carry the hot water from outside in the house and up the stairs to the bathroom, quite a job. We had to heat water in the boiler in the wash house and carry it in buckets to the bathroom to fill the bath which was very old.

The bathroom toilet had no septic tank outside to deal with sewage, just a pit covered in with a large stone slab, which every so often my dad had to remove, it must have been horrible for him, but that was how it was".

Sanitation and Hygiene

The sanitary conditions and hygienic habits of some Linwoodonians in the 19th and early 20th Centuries left nothing to be desired, and often led to the spread of disease and fever.

The *Glasgow Herald* reported on the 27 of April 1872 that Kilbarchan Parochial Board were informed of a fever spreading *"something like an epidemic form"* in an area of the village known as the 'Black Land'. The Board then instructed the Sanitary Inspector and Medical Officer to arrange the removal of the reluctant patents to the infirmary of the infected houses for the purpose of *"cleaning and fumigation"* to *"take the most effectual means in their power to have these objects carried out"*.

The *Paisley & Renfrewshire Gazette* reported on the 01st of December 1900 about a *"cleaning duties of tenants"* case heard in the Paisley Sheriff Court the previous Monday against three men residing in four cottages known as Barrowman's Pit Houses, or Cottages (where T-Junction of Melrose Avenue is today). They were charged with an infringement of Section 31 of the Public Health (Scotland) Act, 1801, *"in so far as the privies and the approaches thereto connected with the cottages were, in the opinion of the Sanitary Inspector, in such a state as to be a nuisance for want of proper cleansing. The respondents pleaded not guilty, but after proof the Sheriff found were fined each in 5s each."*

The *Dundee Evening Telegraph* reported on the 31st of August 1921 about an *"Ejectment Decree"* against a tenant due to the unsanitary conditions of the house she lived in. She was the wife of a Pig Breeder and had continued to occupy a house after it had been uncertified fit for habitation due to not having a water supply and sanitary conveyance. The lady told the court that *"if they put her out, she'd have to go into the fields as she could get no house, and hadn't had a doctor in years"*. She was duly fined £1 and £1 5s expenses.

By the mid-20th Century many of the buildings put up in Victorian times were being demolished and the original village was being expanded with new high quality two-storey houses being built along what became Hart Street, Bridge of Weir and Green Farm Roads, and their surrounds. However, it was in the early 1960's with the huge expansion of modern SSHA built houses that living conditions improved on a large scale. None of the new houses and flats had coal fires and chimneys; all heating would be electric many with storage heaters, and some of them had under-floor central heating. Hot water was provided via immersion boilers.

Initially, when families first moved in to their newly built homes, there were some complaints about one of their apartments being merely a box-room, the conditions of roads and footpaths being incomplete and dirty, and of shops being too far away. But all-in-all, living conditions had greatly improved. The rental cost of a four-apartment house in 1963 was £10 a month, plus 35s for a lock-up garage.

The State of the Streets

A visitor to Linwood from Paisley reported in the 'Round the County' section of the *Paisley & Renfrewshire Gazette* on the 05th of May 1900, on the condition of Linwood's only two streets, as well as our choice of football venue.

"How is it that the streets, if such they may called, of Linwood are always in so dirty a state when I see them? Broken earthenware, tin cans, old paper, and other symbols of rubbish have made themselves uncommonly conspicuous on the occasion of my visits. And I might suggest, so long as I am on Linwood, that the young men of the place who seem to do nothing but play, or try to play, football, might select a more suitable spot for their recreation than the main thoroughfare."

The Arts
James Knox

James Knox was a handloom weaver by trade during his life duration between 1783-1863 and originally hailed from Paisley. However, around the age of forty he moved from Paisley and continued to reside in Linwood, where he became well-known and maintained a quiet and unobtrusive life, until his death.

James's claim to fame and connection with Linwood was that when living in Paisley he worked alongside Paisley's weaver poet Robert Tannahill in the same workshop and was intimately acquainted with him. James took much pleasure in relating his personal recollections of the unhappy Robert Tannahill to the Linwood folks and warmly defended the poet's character against the statements sometimes made to the prejudice of his mural conduct, remarking that Robert Tannahill never exposed himself to the charge of laxity of principles in regard to his intercourse with womankind, whose charms he has so frequently extolled in the purest and sweetest strains of exalted poetry, and that *"he was a good-hearted chiel"*. James used to describe the poet's dress, the chief features of which were his corduroy breeches, terminating at the knees, and his 'rig and ur' stockings. The story told of Robert Tannahill, is that he was in the habit of jotting down his 'coming fancies' as he sat at his loom, was often corroborated by James, who well remembered the ink-bottle and pen, which always stood convenient to the poet, that he would frequently cease playing his shuttle to make use of in giving his ideas a 'local habitation and a name'. James was a great lover of Robert Tannahill's songs, and, being in possession of a good voice, he often entertained his friends in Linwood village by singing with much heartiness and effect some of his old comrade's most popular effusion. The songs, however, which he liked best to sing were ' The *'Braes o' Gleniffer'* and *'Thou Bonnie Wood of Craigielea'*, the tune of which was later modified to form the music for the famous Australian bush folk song and unofficial National Anthem *Waltzing Matilda*.

It seems that both Robert Tannahill and Robert Burns had a lot in common in using their poetic skills in the wooing of women, or as some may see it, in philandering.

Jeff Torrington

Like many Linwood people, Jeff Torrington arrived in the early 1970's to work on the production line of the *Chrysler* Car Plant. He was born in Govan in 1935, where he was brought up and where he would get the reading bug from attending the local McNeil Street library, and then began practicing writing short stories to entertain his wee brother.

After being made redundant from the Car Plant in 1981, and at 47 years of age he was unable to find work and was soon afterwards diagnosed with *Parkinson's Disease*. This led to twelve months of depression, which he snapped out of by throwing himself into completing the novel that would in the end would have taken him 30 years to write. He had realised that writing was the only way he could earn, so intensively, he wrote 2,000 words a day, which became seven drafts. He would have kept on going, but his friend James Kelman said that it was now perfect, and took it to his own publishers, *Secker & Warburg*, for prompt acceptance.

The black comedy novel *Swing Hammer Swing* was published in 1992 and won the Whitbread Prize for Best First Novel, which came along with a cheque for £20,000. This was followed up by a book called *The Devil's Carousel*, a book of short stories on the fictional 'Centaur Car Company's plant in Glasgow'.

Marie Hay

Linwood painting artists Marie Hay of Erskinefauld Road, trained as a graphic designer at Glasgow College of Building and Printing but has always pursued the creative side of her talent with art. She developed a strong interest in Paisley and Glasgow townscapes, which she sketched in, oils, ink and watercolours pastels. Among the scenes she has captured in her impressionistic style are Paisley Abbey, the Halftime School, the Russell Institute, the Coats Observatory, the Town Hall, and a Causeyside Street Back Court, as well as other well-known Paisley scenes.

Marie's sketches have been displayed the Paisley Museum and Art Galleries, the Paisley Library, the University of the West of Scotland Library, The University of Arizona, as well as in the Bar Point and Hamish's pubs in Paisley.

In 1999 Marie opened her own business and studio at Abbeymill in Paisley, where she worked on Art Commissions.

Agnes Thomson

In 1996 the work of a Linwood artist called Agnes Thomson was displayed at an exhibition in the Linwood Community Library in Ardlamont Square along with seventeen other local artists from Linwood and Houston. Not so remarkable you may think, however, this particular artist was soon to be ninety years old and had only picked up a paintbrush for the first time at the age of seventy-nine, just over ten years previously.

Agnes took up art when her husband died, and, because she was at a loose-end she decided to go to St. Brendan's High School when in her 80's where she sat in on classes with the pupils and then sat the Higher Art exam, which she passed, and continued her study and practice at the art class in the Community Centre in Brediland Road.

Margery Ferguson ran a shop called Artizan in the Linwood regional shopping centre in the 1980's and 1990's, which provided arts and craft materials for local artists.

Aileen McLaughlin

Aileen hails of Merchiston Avenue in Linwood. I grew up beside her, our houses being just about 50 yards apart, and I remember us playing 'tents' when we were very young. A few years later she was belting out songs performing at the nearby Tweedie Halls and even bought ABBA records with her pocket-money.

When she had grown up Aileen spent some time in South Africa and London, and then became the a backing singer for Lisa Stansfield and Tom Jones's band in the 1990's, and toured the world with them. She even appeared with Tom on the Royal Variety Performance. Then, in 1998 she got her big break when she landed the role of *Agnetha* in the world's biggest ABBA tribute band *Bjorn Again*. Apart from having a great voice, she had the long legs and blond hair too, so a perfect fit.

In 1998, although still with *Bjorn Again*, Aileen was picked by the worlds' biggest band at the time, the *Spice Girls*, to step-in for *Geri Halliwell*, who had just left the band, in their two-night concerts at Wembley Stadium.

David Miller Bronze Abstract Sculpture

The Phoenix Bronze Abstract Sculpture was commissioned by *Renfrew District Council* in 1968 after Edinburgh artist David Miller won the set competition judged by a panel of experts. They concluded that the winning entry was *"a well-balanced composition of excellent proportions"*. The 11-foot sculpture cost £4,000 and was said to be *"symbolic, displaying both static and dynamic, and representing the artist's view 'of both the past and the future in relation to each *other, of the past and of the future to come"*. The sculpture was cast in bronze at Charles Henshaw's foundry in Edinburgh and erected in Ardlamont Square within the new shopping centre, next to the new library, in early March 1971.

When the shopping centre was to be demolished in 2013 it was carefully removed and stored. It is likely that it was repaired at this time as much damaged had been done to it over the years, i.e., the vertical copper tubes had been sawn off and the main body of the sculpture had a corner sawn off. In 2014 it was re-installed just 100m from its original site, this time outside the new library and Tweedie Halls in the newly opened shopping and town centre development.

The Phoenix Sculpture in its original site in Ardlamont Square after its original installation in early 1971.

The Phoenix Sculpture in its original site in Ardlamont Square, photographed in 2008. Damage likely occurred from scrap metal prospectors clearly evident in that the vertical tubes and corner of main body are sawn-off.

Community Organisations
The Good Templars Lodge

The 'Independent Order of Good Templars' (IOGT) was a total abstinence temperance organisation that campaigned for prohibition and strove to provide social facilities that served non-alcoholic beverages, and also assisted the poor. The IOGT opened a Lodge in Linwood village on 22nd of November 1902 when twenty-three candidates were duly initiated. It was agreed that the lodge be called 'Hope of Linwood' and would meet every Thursday evening in Band Hall in Napier Street. The organisation proved extremely popular in Scotland because of its uncompromisingly prohibitionist aims, its admission of women on an equal footing to men and its extensive provisions for juvenile lodges and education.

For a short period of years from 1897 until early 20th Century, there was also a similar such organisation, the 'St. Andrew Order Reformed Templars Order', which formed the' Linwood Victoria Lodge', and met on Tuesday nights at the Band Hall in Napier Street.

Linwood Conservative Association

In early August 1885, at a meeting of those favourable to Conservative principles in this district was held in the Old Schoolroom. Mr. Andrew Scott of Clippers' House presided. It was resolved to form a Conservative Association, and Mr. Andrew Scott was elected president and Mr. Robert Stevenson secretary. At the close, about 100 were enrolled as members. The organisation would go on to meet regularly at the Club Rooms at No. 1 Napier Street in Linwood village.

Linwood Co-operative Society Limited

Founded in 1872 in Linwood village, this organisation had its first store at No. 32 Napier Street. By the 20th Century they moved to the west side of Bridge Street at the Greenhill Terrace two-storey tenement, and built a new shop on that shite in the 1960's after it had been demolished. It lasted in the 1970's when another supermarket chain took over the shop.

The Co-op had a dividend scheme whereby members were given a unique membership number, which they gave to the cashier at the till when their shopping was completed. Members were rewarded with 4p in the pound cashback each time based on the amount they spent, and this added up over the year. At the end of the year, they could cash-in their dividend, which many did nearer Christmas time.

Craigends Masonic Lodge No. 1042

In 1907, John Charles Cunninghame, of Craigends Estate, became one of the many benefactors in the establishment of a Masonic Lodge in the area. In addition to a financial donation, he also allowed the proposed Lodge to use his family estate's name.

The Aberdeen Press and Journal reported on Friday the 08th of May 1908 that a quarterly meeting the Grand Lodge of Scottish Freemasonry was held the previous afternoon in the Freemasons' Hall, Edinburgh. The Grand Committee made several recommendations, one of which was the recommendation that new charter should be granted to Lodge Craigends, Linwood, Renfrewshire East. This recommendation was duly agreed to.

A ceremony of the cutting of the first sod for the laying of the new village masonic hall was held on the Monday the 08th of June 1908. The new Linwood Masonic Lodge will be called 'The Craigends, Linwood, No. 1042', and will hold their business meetings in the village hall, on Bridge Street, in due course.

On Saturday afternoon on the 21st of November 1908, some two hundred brethren met in the Linwood Public Schoolroom in Napier Street in Linwood to take part in the consecration ceremony of the new Lodge 'Craigends No. 1042'. Having been marshalled in processional order by Bros. Jamie Hunter, jun., and Daniel McMath. Prov. Grand Marshals, the detachments marched to the new hall at west Bridge Street headed by a silver band. The hall, by the way, which is specious and well-appointed as a Lodge-room, had been erected through the energy of the founders of the Lodge, and at a cost of £800. Bro. John M'Kellar, Pro. O.D. of C., proclaimed the Craigends Lodge, No. 1,012, duly constituted a *"regular Lodge of free and accepted Masons"* and Bros. John Gilmartin, gardener to Lady Anne Spiers, was appointed Craigends first Right Worshipful Master.

On Monday the Tuesday 20th of April 1909, St. Mirren hosted new Glasgow Cup holders Queens Park in a match organised in aid of the Linwood Masonic Building Fund.

Freemasonry is a brotherhood based on Christian morality and Lodge Craigends has shown this in its contributions to the needy and many local charities over the years. Craigends Social Club (the social arm of Lodge Craigends) has become a valuable facility which is used by many members of the local community.

Linwood Penny Savings Bank

In Scotland, a comprehensive network of 213 'penny banks' for the very poor, comprised some 60,000 depositors transferring £20,000 a year to the parent Glasgow Savings Bank by 1881. Like many towns and villages in Scotland, Linwood had its own branch during the last quarter of the 19th century.

Horticultural & Gardening

During the late 18th and early 19th Centuries the 'Linwood Horticultural Society' and 'Linwood Thistle Lodge' of the 'The Ancient Order of Free Gardeners Scotland' operated out of the Band Hall in Napier Street, the latter of which based their rituals on freemasonry and even had their secrets and their degrees to complete. Flower Shows were a frequent event and often held at Linwood Public School by the society. People of all classes attended, including such notables Thomas G. Coates of the Paisley based thread empire, and John Galbraith of the Grocery chain family, who submitted exhibits. Prizes were given out various categories of plants and vegetables, for professionals and amateurs alike.

Linwood Flute Band

The Linwood Flute Band were founded around 1875 and seem to only have lasted several years. They often accompanied day excursions to places the Ayrshire coast and Craigends Estate and organised by schools and local employers such as *R & W Watson Papermakers*. However, it seems that they were more than just a social band, as reported in the *Paisley Daily Express* reported on the 12th of July 1880 - *"ORANGEMEN.—On Saturday morning the Orangemen of this town, numbering about 50, headed by the Linwood Flute Band, playing the irate strains of the "Boyne," marched to the station, thence per 11 a.m. train to Glasgow. They returned about seven o'clock in the evening. No disturbance is reported."*

Children's Organisations

Throughout the 20th Century and into the 21st, universal groups such as the Scouts, Boys Brigade and Girl Guides have operated in Linwood at various locations. In the 1950's the Scots had a tin-hut at the west end of Bridge Street. The Scouts and Girl Guides operated out of the old tin-hut hospital in Muirhead Drive in the 1960's, then the latter moved on to the Baptist church. The Boys Brigade originally met in the old parish church before moving to the new moved on to parish church.

McAuley School of Dancing initially operated out of the tin-hut hospital in Muirhead Drive in the 1960's, then, when the Tweedie Halls opened in 1971, they moved there, and stayed there right through to the 1990's.

Entertainment and Social Activities
Children's Activities and Entertainment

During the 19th Century children would on special occasions like Christmas be treated to party's put-on in the school-house thanks to the benevolence of local dignitaries such as Thomas Spier of Blackstoun, Mrs Scott of Clippens House, Mr George W. Richardson the proprietor of the *Cotton Mill*, and later *Messrs R & W Watson* proprietor of the Paper Mill. These parties provided them with tea and buns, sweets, oranges, apples, and they would sing along with the Minister, and enjoy Magic Lantern shows. And nearing the end of the event the Christmas tree would be stripped of its toys and distributed to the three or four hundred children in attendance. On other occasions a 'lucky bag' was produced and there was a draw for prizes from the Christmas tree and all the children won something to take home with them.

And sometimes the children would get the chance to travel away for the day. One such example was reported in the *Paisley Herald and Renfrewshire Advertiser* on the 12th of June 1875, regarding the annual Sabbath School Excursion which took place the previous Saturday:

"The scholars, numbering 300, with their teachers, headed by the Linwood Flute Band, marched to Craigends House, where, in presence of J. C. Cunninghame, the whole company sung a hymn, after which they were welcomed to visit all the policies and gardens, which having done, they marched to Nether Craigends, where they were regaled by Mrs White and family with buns, milk, &c."

At the beginning of the 20th Century entertainment for children was sometimes both social and educational. One such example was reported in the *Paisley & Renfrewshire Gazette* on the 17th of November 1906, was as follows:

"Lime-Light Lecture - On Friday evening last, Mr J. M. B. Taylor, Paisley, delivered a lime-light lecture is the Public School, Linwood, entitled "A Ramble Around Linwood." Mr Taylor threw on the screen a great many local views of the village and surrounding district taken by himself during last summer. The lecture was much

appreciated by the audience and proved both instructive and enjoyable. Many of the views were exceedingly picturesque, and the views of the surrounding landscape were much admired. Mr Taylor also gave much useful information on nature studies around the district, and pointed out many peculiarities regarding trees and insect life he bad noticed in his rambles. Mr McEwan gave a short address on "Astronomy," illustrated by diagrams thrown on the screen, and also by a novel invention of his own showed the positions of the planetary systems on an ordinary umbrella. Mr W. J. H. Reid, in thanking the lecturer, pointed out the benefit of such lecture and hoped that the School Board would see their way next winter to inaugurate a course of such lectures from the educational standpoint as in his opinion the method of imparting instruction was a valuable one."

During the 2nd half of the 20th Century, especially after Linwood's vast expansion with many new incomers, children had many choices, as explained in other sections of this book. As well as attending social organisations such as the Boys Brigade, Boy Scouts, Dancing Classes, and Girls Guides, they had sports to play, and the environment around them to explore. And at weekends they could go to the likes of the swimming baths, film shows, and the cinema.

In late 1960's and early 1970's there were bus-run trips down to the Ayrshire coast organised by Linwood Parish Church for mothers and their children. I vividly remember travelling on the bus with everybody signing *"the front of the bus they cannae sing, they cannae sing, for peanuts"*, and getting the appropriate response from the front of the bus gang. And singing other songs of the day like *"chirpy chirpy, cheep cheep"*.

From the 1970's most children were taken on holidays within the UK by their families, and by the 1980's some were lucky enough go on foreign holidays to Europe, both with their schools and with their families.

Adult Activities and Entertainment

19th Century

During the 19th Century socialising with entertainment was put-on by the various community organisations, most of which were held in the Band Hall and Old School Room in Napier Street. The *Paisley Daily Express* on the 03rd of January 1880, reported on one such event, as follows:

"Festival Of Messrs Storer & Sons Workers. - Last night, through the generosity of Messrs Storer & Sons, cotton spinners, late of Thorn, Johnstone, and now of Linwood, the employees in these extensive works, with special friends from Linwood, Johnstone, Paisley, &c., engaged in what turned out to be a most successful and happy gathering of about 300."

On the 16th of June 1883 the *Paisley & Renfrewshire Gazette* reported on an excursion arranged for its employees, by the *Clippens Oil Company*, as follows:

"On Saturday, the employees at Clippens Oil Works had their annual excursion to Rothesay. The workers, to the number of about 500, marched to Linwood, where the Caledonian Company had made arrangements for running a special passenger train over their goods line for the accommodation of the excursionists. On arriving at Greenock, the steamer Athole was awaiting them to convey them to Rothesay, where a very pleasant day was spent. The firm, with their usual liberality, put the trip within the means of all."

Other mining related companies and the Cotton Mills would also arrange annual excursions down the Ayrshire coast for their employees.

First Half of the 20th Century

As with the 19th Century, during the first half of the 20th Century socialising with entertainment was put-on by the various community organisations, most of which were held in the Band Hall and Old School Room in Napier

Street. The *Paisley & Renfrewshire Gazette* on the 17th of November 1906, reported on one such event, as follows:

"On Friday evening of last week, a most successful social and dance was held in the Schoolroom, Linwood, under the auspices of the Hope of Linwood Lodge, [International Order of Good Templars]. After tea, which was purveyed in excellent style, the musical part of the programme was ably sustained by several attendees, all of whom were enthusiastically received. After the usual votes of thank had been moved and responded to, the room was cleared, and dancing was indulged in till an early hour in the morning."

On the 29th of June 1907 the *Paisley & Renfrewshire Gazette* reported on an excursion arranged for its employees, by the *Eclipse Tool Company*, as follows:

"An Enjoyable Trip. On Saturday last, the employees of the Eclipse Tool Company, numbering between thirty and forty, accompanied by a few friends, celebrated their second annual excursion, generously given by their employers. The party left Houston Crosslee at 8.06am for Greenock, from there to Millport via Rothesay. After a very pleasant day spent in Millport with most favourable weather, the company left for home at 7.30 via Fairlie Pier, the trip home forming a very enjoyable circular tour."

Second Half of the 20th Century

With the massive injection of people to the population of Linwood from 1963 when the car plant opened, facilities were soon created for masses to socialise and be entertained. The village, which in recent years had just two pubs, by 1972 had four pubs, with *The Clippens Inn* opening in western Linwood in 1973. Linwood's only hotel, *The Golden Pheasant*, opened in 1967. However, the biggest change, in terms of entertainment, were the four social clubs that opened in the early 1970's.

Members of the Rangers Supporters Social Club hold their first dance of the season in the Tweedie Halls – circa 1971.

International acts were coming to Linwood's social clubs; singers such as *Tony Christie* and *Matt Monro*; bands such as *Guys and Dolls* and *The Drifters*. And in the case of the *The Clippens Inn*, crowds were drawn in from all over Renfrewshire due to the top Disc Jockeys from Radio Clyde hosting the Disco's there.

Members and staff of the St Brendan's Social Club enjoying their night - circa 1971/72.

The closure of the car plant would obviously have a knock-on effect, as a change in social culture, and so by the early 1990's *The Golden Pheasant* had closed, and others, pubs and clubs, would follow over the next three decades.

By 2023 there were only two pubs left operating in Linwood, the Clippens Inn and the Heritage. And in terms of Social Clubs, the Peter Scarff, the Welfare and Recreational, and the Masonic Social Clubs were only open part-time, mainly at weekends. This was likely due to two reasons, affordability to the high costs of living, but also because there had been a steady change in culture over the previous three decades whereby people had become less sociable, not just in Linwood, but all over the country.

Chronological Timeline of Pubs and Clubs

In 1847 the Paisley Presbytery noted from the last census in 1841 the number of Public Houses in the towns and villages of the various parishes. In the case of Linwood village, with a population of 1,126 people, there were five Public Houses. Twelve years later on the 17th of December 1853, *The Commonwealth (Glasgow) newspaper* reported that a group from the Paisley Abstainers League had *"visited Linwood on the Monday evening, and addressed a crowd meeting on the subject of temperance. A society was formed with 68 members, which number has since increased to 86. There are five public-houses in the village, but neither a book-seller, nor a baker"*.

Most of the five public houses mentioned above are likely to be those detailed below, but there could have been others. These public houses closed at 9pm daily.

Drinking Establishments 19th Century and 1st Half of the 20th Century

Houston's Bar: At No. 19 Napier Street, where Corals Bookmakers is today, which would later become the

Tavern Bar in the first half of the 20th Century up until 1964. It was owned by Mr William Houston.

The Black Bull Inn: At No. 23 Bridge Street, near corner with Hart Street, had been there since at least the mid-19th Century. Locals knew it as 'Burn's Pub'. Patrick Smythe was the last owner before he had it demolished and built a new pub in its place called the *Ponderosa Bar*.

The Bucks Head Inn: At No. 16 Bridge Street, on corner of the south side of [wee] Napier Street, at Linwood Cross - had a hotel license and had been there since at least the mid-19th Century - demolished in the mid-1950's. In 1857 it was the property of Robert Donald from Paisley, with Francis Best being the Publican.

The Stag Inn: Was situated as the 2nd building on right when entering the north side of Napier Street from Linwood Cross. In 1857 it was the property of the occupants and owners James Inglis and William Millar.

Gardiner's Public House: At No. 25 Bridge Street was known to be in business in the 2nd half of the 19th Century. It was owned by Alexander Gardener, but in 1877 was sold to David Robertson for £1,290, and so became *Robertson's Public House*.

Cowan's Public House: This business is mentioned in an 1891 newspaper article as a public-house in Linwood, but it's exact location, in either Bridge or Napier streets, is unknown, as it whether it was a separate establishment, or in the same premises of one of those listed above.

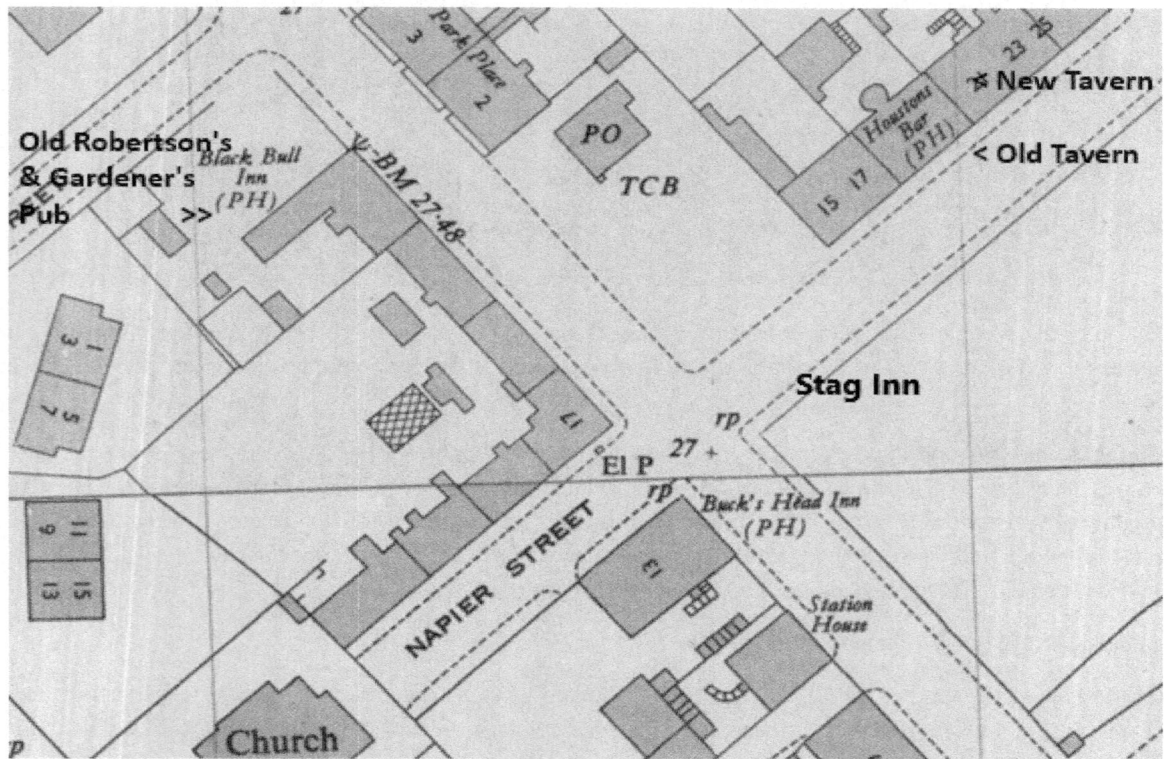

Mid-20th Century plan showing the village pubs of the past (Stag Inn, old Tavern, Roberston's/Gardener's), present (Black Bull, Buck's Head Inn, Houston's), and future (new Tavern). The location of Cowan's Public House is unknown; possible precursor of Houston's or Stag Inn.

Drinking Establishments of the 2nd half of the 20th Century until today

There was a transition of drinking establishments after the opening of the Car Plant and the expansion of the population of Linwood in the mid-1960's. The Buckshead Inn had been demolished in the 1950's, the Black Bull in 1964, and the Tavern had moved to new premises next door in 1964. But new establishments were to be built, as detailed below.

The Rootes Club: Opened in 1963 on Linwood Road near the Toll – became *Chrysler Club* in 1966 - Closed mid-1970's

The Rangers Supporters Social Club: Opened in 1974 at No. 11 Napier Street – was forced to close in 1985, and then re-opened as the Linwood Welfare and Recreational Social Club in 1987 - remains opened today.

The St Conval's Social Club: Opened at Christmas 1971 at the start of Candren Road and changed to the Peter Scarff Social Club in 2022 (after 3 years closure due to Covid-19 Pandemic) - remains opened today.

The Craigends Social Club Lounge: Opened around 1970 on the west end of Bridge Street and is still going part-time today.

The St Brendan's Social Club: Opened in early 1970's on Stirling Drive - Closed 2007

The Ponderosa Bar: Opened on the 17th of December 1965 on Bridge Street near Linwood Cross, became the 'Brandy Burn' for a few years in the 1980's, then became 'The Heritage' - remains opened today.

The Golden Pheasant Hotel: Opened 1967 at the beginning of Moss Road - Closed 1993

The Tavern Bar: Opened at No. 19 Napier Street around 1967 – Closed December 2022

The Venture Bar: Opened 1972 at the east end of Bridge Street - Closed Friday the 13th of December 2002

The Clippens Inn: Opened 1974 at 57 Clippens Road – Snug and Lounge removed to become supermarket around 2010 – the bar remains opened today.

This 1930's grainy aerial image shows the Buckshead Inn in the centre at Linwood Cross, with Goods Yard and Linwood Parish Chruch in the background.

This early 1960's aerial image shows the Black Bull Inn in the centre near the corner of Hart Street, with barber shop adjoining it, then the huts of Linwood Clinic and Starks chemist.

The Golden Pheasant opened on the 23rd of March 1967. It closed as a hotel in the late 1993 had other uses before being demolished in the early 2000's.

The Clippens Inn opened in 1974. The bar remains today, but the big function/disco lounge and snug were converted into a supermarket around 2010.

Paisley Daily Express - Tuesday 29 April 1986: Regulars at the Tavern Bar Linwood give owner Frank Lee a cheer at he breaks the bottle of coins - a total of £159 spilled out. The cash went towards the Tavern's old age pensioners' fund.

Christmas Party Held in the Chrysler car factory circa around 1973 (provided by Jim Brady, who is included in the photo).

St Conval's Film Club held in the in the Tweedie Halls on Saturday mornings – circa 1971.

Sport
Linwood Football Teams

The earliest known record of organised football in Linwood was reported by the *Paisley Daily Express* on the 06th of May 1880, thus:

"Linwood - Football —A match was played at Linwood last night between the 3rd Linwood and 1st Redan Ramblers, and after a very interesting game resulted in favour of the former by three goals to none."

Linwood District Football Clubs - in Chronological Order

Inkermann Rangers FC: This clubs' period of existence is unclear, but there are records of them having played between the years of 1881-1910. They won the *Paisley and District League* and Cup in seasons 1908/9 and repeated the feat one year later.

Clippens F.C. were founded in 1882, their colours were all-white, and they played at Moss Park. They joined the Scottish Football Association almost immediately and played in the 1883–84 Scottish Cup. Before the 1884–85 season, Clippens took over the *Linwood F.C.* club (who also played in all-white, at Craig Park, and became defunct in 1984), but despite this did not survive the season. By 1885, it had a mere 30 members, half of its total after its first season and as the club did not pay its subscription to the *Scottish Football Association*, so was struck off the membership roll before the 1885–86 season, which meant it could not enter the Scottish Cup. The club was replaced in Linwood the following season by *Clippens Athletic*, which suffered an abject humiliation in the Renfrewshire Cup, with a 24–0 defeat to Neilston - made even worse by Neilston starting the match with just nine men.

Linwood Myrtle F.C. / Linwood Thistle: This club decided to change name from the former, to the latter in September 1899 at a meeting in the "Bucks Head Hall". However, it is not known when they were formed. Linwood Thistle continued playing until around 1952 and then went defunct. In 1991, Linwood's John McCallum created a club of the same name to play in the *Paisley and District League*, but without realising he had effectively resurrected the club, as informed by his wife Carol. In 2015 they were still playing.

Linwood Victoria [aka Vics]: This clubs' period of existence is unclear, but they definitely played between the years of 1899-1928. Homes games were played at Anchor Park in Linwood. Although the park's location in unknown.

Linwood Harp: This clubs' period of existence is unclear, but there are records of them having played between the years of 1906-11.

St. Conval's: The original St Conval's played in the first class Under 21 Juvenile League from around 1926 until the 1980's, when they changed to boys' clubs and youth football was formed. The only connection with the current youth club, which started in the 1970's, and is still going, is the name. Separately from these teams was a youth team called St Conval's Boys Guild, which was started in the 60s and lasted around 10 years.

Linwood St Conval's Boys Club at Linwood Public Park – Photo circa 1969/70 (by Jim McCallum's father William). Back Row: Jock Reid (adult), Jim Heron, William Agnew, Brian Carrol, Peter Scarff, John Dougan, Eddie O'Flynn, Daniel Heron (adult). Front Row: Billy Gamble, John McGugan, Arthur Sherry, Gerry Docherty, William Dundas, Jim McCallum, William Scarff.

Rangers Sports Club (RSC) **/ Rangers Youth Club** (RYC) **/ Linwood Rangers F.C.** (LRFC) **/ Linwood Rangers Youth F.C. 2006** (LRYFC). This club began around 1967. It has since morphed from one incarnation to another. Professional Player Maurice Johnson, of Celtic and Rangers infamy, played for RYC in the 1977/78 season, as he had cousins that lived in Linwood's Abernethy Drive.

Linwood Rangers Youth Club at Kilbarchan Public Park – Circa 1978. Back Row: Mr Billy Meikle (Manager), Grant Hooper, Gavin White, Robert Brackenbridge, David Adam, Mark Finlay, Brian Bellingham, Maurice Johnston, Gerry O'Leary. Front Row: Charlie Parsons, Joe Miller, Peter Darroch, Sammy Simpson, Robert Burns. George Meikle.

Watson's [Paper Mill] Football Club: played in the 1960's and up to 1986, at the Reid Gear Park, when they became **Linwood United Taxis Club**, and continued on until around 1993, then changed name to **St Brendan's**, their new sponsor, and finished around 1995.

Reid Gear [Engineering]: aka Reid Gear Spurs, had a football team in the 1970's/80's and played home games at their own Reid Gear Park.

Linwood United Football Club: played during the 1970's. They had been set-up to have no religious allegiances, as other local clubs may have had.

Football Pitches

The central place for playing football games over the years was the Public Park. However, various newspaper articles from the late 19th and early part of the 20th Centuries reported on football matches being played at such locations in the Linwood district such as 'Craig Park' (Linwood F.C.), 'Muirhead Park' (Linwood Thistle). 'Anchor Park' (Linwood Victoria), and 'McLean Park' (St. Conval's), but the whereabouts of these parks are unknown. Known football parks were located at the Public Park, the start of Middleton Road where Linwood Thistle played, a park on the south side of Linwood Parish Church, and a park just off the left-hand side of the Barochan Road adjacent to Johnstone North Railway station.

Professional Football Players from Linwood - in Chronological Order

Start Year	Players Names	Start Year	Players Names
1887	Tom Brandon	1986	Jimmy Smith
1920	Charlie Pringle	1987	John Hillcoat
1928	Peter Scarffe	1988	Jim Arthur
1931	Tom Wylie	1988	Steven Logan
1937	John Gilmartin	1989	Peter Feeney
1946	John McGrory	1990	Martin McGarvey
1957	Pat Liney	1991	Malky Thomson
1965	John Kelly "Dixie" Deans	1994	Steven McDougall
1968	Eddie Moore	1998	Alan Reid
1969	Billy Kellock	1998	Neil Scally
1975	Billy Thomson	2003	David Lowing
1976	Paul Hendrie	2003	Darryl Duffy
1977	Jacky Keay	2005	Adam Moffat
1977	John Docherty	2005	Paul Paton
1978	Andy (Drew) Brannigan	2005	Alan Muir
1988	Jim Arthur	2018	Conor O'Keefe

Other Football Incidentals

The Curtis Trophy was an annual fixture played between St Brendan's High School and Linwood High School. It started in 1975 and was played annually at alternate home grounds, for several years. The Trophy was put up by Mr Robert Curtis, retiring Head teacher of Linwood High School, that year, to prosper good relations between the schools.

In an *Auld Linwood Town & Surrounds* Poll we asked: *"who was the best football player to come out of Linwood, that didn't play professionally?"*. The result was Grant Hooper with 33% of the vote.

'The Wembley Club' gathered outside the Tavern Bar just before they head off to Hampden for a Scotland v England Home International game in 1976. Joe Jordan and Kenny Dalglish scored in the 2-1 victory with the latter humiliating Goalkeeper Ray Clemence by putting the ball through his legs.

Bowling

On the 01st of June 1871 Linwood got its first Bowling Green. The *North British Daily Mail* reported on it four days later thus:

"Linwood – Opening of a New Bowling Green. In Linwood and neighbourhood, the want of some innocent recreative amusement for summer evenings, have long been felt by a number of gentlemen, and a short time ago it was resolved to establish a bowling club, and provide green to supply that want. George Ronaldson, Esq. of Linwood Mills, was chosen as president for the club, and the membership rapidly increased till it now numbers about fifty gentlemen. The opening proceedings commenced on Saturday afternoon, about four o'clock, when there assembled, besides the members, a large number of the villagers, and deputations from Wellmeadow, Charleston, Bank End, Victoria, and Abercorn Bowling Clubs of Paisley, and also from Kilbarchan Club. Mr Ronaldson, in declaring the green opened, congratulated all present on meeting together on such an auspicious event for the village of Linwood. Thereafter the members and their friends engaged in friendly games."

Mr Ronaldson also built a Pavilion and Bowling House at his own expense and provided gas for heating purposes so that it could be used as a Reading Room in the winter. The Pavilion and Bowling House were described by an early visitor as *"rather pretty corrugated pavilion and house, lined with wood inside"*.

The exact location of this bowling green is no longer known, but it was certainly in the village. However, there are clues. A newspaper article of 1872 advertising the sale of a two-story tenement building, gives its location as being *"on the south side of Napier Street, immediately to the west of the bowling green."* The Watson's

Paisley Directory of 1889-1890 gives the bowling clubs' address as No. 1 Bridge Street. From this we can perhaps deduct that it was on the south side of Bridge Street behind the buildings that fronted it.

The replacement bowling green was opened on the 12th of July 1902 by Mrs Horsburgh, who performed the opening ceremony amidst the pouring rain, by throwing the first jack and bowls, which she was photographed doing. A short game of five ends followed and a photograph of the whole company was taken at the end, which included some visitors.

The very same bowling clubs continues today at the same site at the north end of Napier Street.

There is also the Woodlands Community Bowling Club, off Brediland Road, which was formed in 1984.

Quoiting

This game is a combination of bowls and discuss, and requires both brawn and brain. It was a game played initially by miners in the Linwood district since mining began there in the mid-19th Century.

The *Port-Glasgow Express* reported on the 22nd of February 1895 on the 'Quoiting – Formation of a League for Renfrewshire:

"Considerable interest was taken in the meeting of representatives from the different quoiting clubs in Renfrewshire, which was convened in Globe Hotel, Paisley, on Wednesday. There were sixteen gentlemen present, representing the various town of Renfrewshire. The meeting went into a code of rules very heartily, and after some discussion they were formed and adopted. Linwood played its first game the following month and became very proficient at the game, very quickly."

The *Port-Glasgow Express* reported on his very point on the 14th of June the same year:

"Quoiting Note.—To-morrow the Port- Glasgow Quoiting Club will have one of their toughest games of the season. Their opponents are the Linwood, who have an unbroken record in the Renfrewshire League competitions. The match takes place on the ground in the Public Park, tour rinks aside, 25 shots up, with a 2l yards' pitch. The game will no doubt attract much attention among local followers of Quoiting."

Several years later, on the 28th of March 1913, the *Scottish Referee* reported *"The Linwood Club is welcomed back to the Association, after being defunct for several years."*

Many years later, on the 25th of August 1989, the *Paisley Daily Express* reported on the game being resurrected in Linwood, and this was all thanks to local historian Jim Winters. Jim had managed to obtain from *Watson Grange Paper Convertors*, the lease of a cottage, a space for a rink, and a covered area for the public to watch, just off Napier Street. Jim had also gotten a team together and they Linwood Quoiting Club played their first game in apparently over 40 years.

The club seems to have stopped playing again in the early 2000's.

Cock-Fighting

The *Paisley & Renfrewshire Gazette* reported on the 12th of November 1892, of a case of cock fighting whereby a promising Linwood Cock took on a champion Johnstone Cock, and came out a worthy champion:

"Alexander Muir went straight to Johnstone and called on James Midwell, who was in joint-partnership over several first-class birds, that were under the charge of cotton spinner in Linwood. Mr. Muir was successful in inducing Mr. Midwell to lend him the best of the lot, on account Muir declaring in strong terms, that there would be no peace in Ewing Street [Kilbarchan] till the Snapper's cock (which was the bully of four) was killed. On the following day this champion from the Linwood was slipped; Mr. Muir and his followers were waiting anxiously to see it come in contact with the Snap's." They soon met in the Bog at the dinner hour, and the fight

lasted some time, the birds being well matched. By-and-bye, however, Stevenson's cock became visibly shaky on its legs, and the tide of victory seemed on Muir's side; and although the "Snap's" bird fought game to the last, the Linwood cock laid it low and crowed over its dead body. It is needless to state that Alexander Muir was overjoyed with 'the downfall of our worthy's bully of four,' which now made the Linwood bird cock of the walk."

Cockfighting had been relatively common in the 18th and 19th Centuries, but was finally banned outright in Scotland in 1895.

Cricket

Linwood [aka Linclive] Cricket Club competed in crickets matches between the years of 1871 and 1878. They would later play in a field provided by farmer Mr William Kerr of Linclive Farm. For his generosity the club presented Mr Kerr with a handsome silver-mounted walking stick on the 20th of November 1875.

Ploughing

Throughout the 19th and early 20th Centuries the farmers of Linwood would take part in the annual County ploughing match, under the auspices the *Renfrewshire Agricultural Society*. Locations would include Linclive Farm and the Farm on the Green.

Foxhunting

Foxhunting was the preserve of the landed gentry, titled Gentlemen and their guests, which included females. The hunts were carried out throughout the surrounding countryside areas of Linwood, including Linwood Moss, Fulwood, Barochan, Houston, Crosslee, Milliken, and Craigends. Its popularity was strongest in the second half of the 19th Century but continued throughout the 20th Century. Indeed, the public house in Houston village has been called the 'Fox and Hounds' for many years and displays stuffed foxes on its interior walls. It seems strange calling 'Foxhunting' a sport today, but it was considered as such, in the past.

Thankfully, Foxhunting in Scotland was consigned to history on the 24th January 2023 when MSPs voted to pass the *Hunting with Dogs (Scotland) Bill*, which replaced the *Protection of Wild Mammals (Scotland) Act 2002*, which had allowed fox hunting to continue much as it did before, due to loopholes in the legislation that were exploited by fox hunting packs.

Cycling

In the latter 19th Century, the *Paisley & Renfrewshire Gazette* regularly featured updates on cycle clubs and their cycle runs all over the west of Scotland, including those of the *Linwood United Cycling Club*. The club began in 1996, had fifty members within a year, and continued through the early part of the 20th Century. They also had a Ladies section, and both men and woman groups met and started their runs from Linwood Cross. Apart from their own training runs, they competed in the *Renfrewshire Cyclists' League*.

In the 1980's/90's, Linwood had two Road Racing Cyclists of note, namely Malcolm Little and Drew Wilson.

Among Malcolm's successes was first place in the Scottish 25-mile Cycling Championship in 1986 at Musselburgh.

Drew was a junior and senior road race cycling champion in the 1980s/90's who turned professional in 1994 after trailing with *Banana/Falcon*, and represented Scotland at the Commonwealth Games in 1986, 1994 & 1998. Among Drew's extensive successes was being the Scottish Road Champion on six occasions. In 2014 Drew launched *VisualBikeFit*, a bespoke bike fitting service in his studio at the foot of the Crow Road in Lennoxtown, which is still going strong today.

Linwood United Cycling Club – circa 1900: George Robinson is featured in this photo somewhere. His Great Nephew Don Kessler from Oregon, USA, provided the photo.

Drew Wilson started off as a schoolboy riding for Johnstone Wheelers in the 1980's, the turned professional and represented Scotland at three commonwealth games

Angling

With Linwood bordered by two rivers, the Black Cart and the Gryfe, there has always been angling activities taking place. However, for much of the 19th and 20th Centuries the rivers were polluted due to emissions from factories being discharged into them.

This was to change from the 1980's with the implementation of new Environmental Laws and Penalties that could be issued. Before long Salmon and Sea Trout began to make runs upstream and were being caught by anglers. These two rivers are managed by the Castle Angling Club and the Abercorn Angling Club respectively.

The St Brendan's Social Club had a Sea Angling Club section, which I was a member of myself in the late 1970's and early 1980's. On Saturday the 16th of December 1989, the biggest disaster to ever hit Linwood occurred when five local men and boys, as well as the skipper from Gourock, were drowned when the 35-foot Prawn Fishing Trawler they were in, sank just 300 yards from Gourock pier. The whole town was devastated. I was particularly shocked for two reasons; reason one being that I knew three of the Linwood locals, as well as the skipper Willie Irving; and reason two because I had tried to go on the trip myself by asking the Boat Convenor George Head if he had any vacant places, when I met him in the *Clippens Inn* bar, the previous Sunday evening. He had said he'd contact my father, with whom he worked, should someone pull out of the trip. I can't explain how I felt when I found out about the disaster.

Linwood's Jimmy Mullen lands a 14' Sand Shark on the beach, after a 4-hour fight – his gold medal is shown in adjacent photo.

As well as this gold, Linwood's Jimmy Mullen also won a bronze medal as part of a 4 Man Scotland Team in the 1978 World Cup in South Africa, for finishing 3rd overall.

Linwood at War
Crimean War

The Battles of the 'Great Redan', 'Balaclava', and 'Inkerman' took place during the Crimean War (1853-56). In the case of the 'Battle of "Balaclava' it witnessed one of the most famous acts of battlefield bravery, the Thin Red Line, and one of the most infamous blunders in military history, the *Charge of the Light Brigade*. During this war and many Scots, including a sizable number from Linwood, fought there for their Queen and Country. The 'Battle of the Great Redan' was a major battle during the Crimean War, fought between British forces against Russia on 18th of June and 8th of September 1855 as a part of the 'Siege of Sevastopol'.

The *Paisley Herald and Renfrewshire Advertiser* reported on the 06th of January, 1855, that *"the sum of £11, 13s, & 9d was contributed by the inhabitants of the village of Linwood"* in aid of the widows and orphans affected by the Crimean War. This Patriotic Fund was set up *By Her Majesty's Command* in October 1854 with Prince Albert as its President. Its purpose was to co-ordinate the collection and distribution of money donated by the public for the widows and orphans of men killed during the Crimean War.

2nd Boer War

The *Paisley & Renfrewshire Gazette* reported on the 17th of March 1900 Corporal Robert Henderson of the Seaforth Highlanders being called-up to the front. Before leaving, he was presented with a sum of money by his fellow-workers in the paper mill.

The same newspaper reported on the 27th of October 1900, just seven months later, on the tragic death of Sergeant R. Henderson as notified by the War Office that week. Robert had been killed in the surprise attack at Jagersfontein on the 16th inst. The news was received in the village with the deepest regret, where he had resided for many years with his friends. Sergeant Henderson was held in much revered character, willing and obliging in his manner, and thus commended himself to all with whom he came in contact. He was in his last years' service as a reservist, and when leaving for the front in April last, he was the recipient of a present from his fellow-workmen. In recent letters received from him had mentioned having been struck by bullets on three different occasions, but thought he would soon be on his way home. There were few soldiers from the Linwood area at the front, and this was the first casualty that had occurred.

The same newspaper reported one year later on two volunteer soldiers from Linwood being called-up to the front in the 2nd Boer War in South Africa. The members and friends of the *Linwood Thistle Football Club* had met in the Buck's Head Hall, on Saturday evening for the purpose of doing honour to two of their number, Privates Peter Grant and George Ross, who are leaving the village for the seat of war in South Africa. These two young men, who were connected with F Company, 2nd V.B.A. and S.H., volunteered for active service at the front over a year ago, and had just been called up to proceed to South Africa.

The Great War (WW1)

Much of the following information in this WW1 section is taken from a set of notes provided to me by the *Linwood War Memorial Association* Team, which in turn came from reports in *The Paisley and Renfrewshire Gazette* from during and just after WWI.

After Britain declared war on Germany on the 04th of August 1914, Linwood was quick to respond to the call from King and Country. In the early months over forty men had left the village, including reservists, recruits, and territorials. Eighteen of these men came from the *Reid Gear Engineering company*, who employed a total of 190 persons workers at that time. By December that year it was reported that fifteen of these men that had joined-up were from Linwood Parish Church, and by January 2015, 23 from St Conval's had joined them. And those left behind contributed from their wages to the European War Fund.

Both Protestant Ministers and the Catholic Archbishop of Glasgow came out urging young men to join-up; this was truly a united response.

The *Johnstone and District Charity Organisation Society* helped with relief given to the wives and dependants of the soldiers, with which their joint honorary secretary Mr W. M. Stevenson (Factor at 36 Napier Street) played a large part.

The families at home looked forward to word from the front, a letter from their loved ones, but dreaded receiving the type of correspondence that confirmed the death of their husbands, sons, and fathers. Such notification was sent in a filled-out B 104-82B Form, and of course, not all men returned. News arrived in the village sporadically of those that had fallen.

Despite these losses, Linwood prospered during the war years, because of the number of war-related contracts won by the firms based there. *Dent & Co & Johnson* gave their workers much overtime as a large number of compasses from torpedo boats and aeroplanes needed repaired.

The introduction of conscription in 1916 changed the working and production situation greatly. Up until this point firms like *Reid Gear* and *Watsons paper mill* had been able to retain adequate male workers to maintain production targets, which was increasingly war-related, but now they struggled to hold on to their employees as they were increasingly called-up. So, women took their places.

Linwood's first ever air raid warning was sounded in 1915 due to a recent Zeppelin scare, and these warnings would continue.

On the 20th of April, 1918, the *Paisley and Renfrew Gazette* reported that £9,644 had been raised by the people of Linwood over just the previous six days as a resulted of an arranged "War Weapons Week". The purpose of this exercise was to generate money to buy Linwood an Anti-Aircraft Gun. This amounted to an investment of £4 10s per head of the population. The newspaper commented that this "shows a spirit worthy of the times". And, because the target amount had been substantially overshot, funds were also provided for a 'Linwood Tank', a 'Linwood Seaplane' and eight 'Linwood Schools' Machine Guns.

At the end of the war, it was reported that thirty-two men were lost in the war from St Conval's Church, twenty from Linwood Parish Church, and three that worshipped at the St John's Episcopal Church in Johnstone. However, this number would later rise.

Many men were mentioned in dispatches, and medals were won, which included several Military Medals and one Victoria Cross.

The *Linwood Heroes Fund* was created to recognise those men belonging to the district who had, by their gallantry, won honours on the field of battle. £90 was raised and at a large gathering of the people of Linwood in the Masonic Hall; the soldiers (six initially) that had been awarded honours by their country, were presented with inscribed gold watches as a token of esteem from the people of the village.

A highly successful concert was given by the pupils of Linwood Public School on the evenings of 27th and 28th March 1919, the proceeds of which amounted to £320. This money was to be devoted to the 'Village War Memorial Fund', but nothing more was ever heard of this fund.

Homes fit for heroes to live in

At the time of the First World War, there were only two streets in Linwood, Napier and Bridge Streets, with the exception of three villas that had been built in Bridge of Weir (B.O.W.) Road in 1914. Many ex-servicemen had returned home to Linwood from WWI to industrial slump and mass unemployment; but Linwood did gain one lasting benefit. In December 1918, Lloyd George had promised the electorate *"homes fit for heroes to live in"* and some, at least, were finally built. Difficulties had still to be overcome, including the proposal to employ a Mining Engineer to inspect and assess the proposed sites. But despite these drawbacks, the houses near the 'wee red school' in B.O.W. Road, were built, and declared ready for occupation on the 04th of June 1921. These houses are the two-storey 'cottage style' flats are still situated in both North and South Drives and also stretching back along B.O.W. Road, towards Bridge Street.

Since no village war memorial was ever built, those houses are Linwood's only public monument to those who died in the *"war to end all wars"*.

A Poem from the Front

Linwood lady Donna Scott provided the following poem written by her Great Uncle, who was a soldier from Linwood, who fought in the trenches of France in 1918.

By Private John McElhoney, S/25019 10th Bt., Argyll and Sutherland Highlanders, France 1918.

I remember so well, the Trysting Tree, and also the Clippens Bing.
I can still see Alleluia's at the place, where they used to sing.
Wee boys on stools would stand up and preach, as men into their pockets would reach.
Abyssinian blood, the fat Italian would scream, as raspberry he poured, onto our ice cream.
Jessie Beastie, poor lady, how sick you were, we were but bairns, and didn't really care.

Hurry up! Said the mill horn, with its plaintive wail, (I've heard the wee bookie has landed in jail).
Old Charlie in his shop had just one leg, no artificial foot, just a wooden peg.
I loved the McCurdys and the Hornes as well, and dear old Paddy, what a tale he could tell.
The Inkerman crowd and the Blackstoun few, these were the people I'm glad that I knew.
We walked all the way to swim in the Gryffe, ah, those were the happiest days of my life.
Or going up the Braes to the Bonnie We Well, a million stories that place could tell.
The school jaunt, remember? The pipes and the cross, all the fun, and those races we ran on the grass.
Cookies and cakes, a tin full of milk, Mrs Costello dressed up in her fine silk,
Dearest Mollie, with whom I went to school, she was so gentle, I was the fool.
The O'Donnells, John Crampsie and big Pat Flynn, to this day I miss you, for you were my kin.
Remember Lizzie Liddles and the old Black Bull, the University of St. Conval's, and the posh public school.
Our Kirk and the Chapel, of which we were proud, as each Sunday they drew a large crowd.
I could write on forever, but now I feel sad, when I think of those days I spent as a lad.
Those wonderful days of my childhood, back home in Scotland, in my dear Linwood.

John also wrote another poem called *What a soldier saw in the Trenches*. He was an Engineer with the *Reid Gear Co. Ltd* and was only 19 when he lost his life, sadly just over three weeks short of the end of the war. His brother Patrick returned from the war and was awarded the Military Medal for saving four wounded comrades.

World War Two

Linwood lady Sarah-Anne Doyle kindly provided me with copies of hand written notes left by her dear Papa John McSporran (1927-2017). In it he recounts his call-up to the army and wartime experiences.

"On my 18th birthday I was called up for the army and sent to a camp in Elgin where I was trained by the Seaforth Highlanders and then by Lovat Scots followed by the Air Borne Troops. Sent by train to Woolwich Arsenal Batteries airwing during an air raid warning by German V-Rocket bombs. This didn't last long. Sent [to] many and varied camps and areas, eventually returned home in 1948. Started back in Paper Mill being paid four pounds a week, being glad to be home live and well. Recalled to the army in 1951 for war in Korea, [but] because of being deaf was discharged from army December 1952. I served 7 years 10 months."

On his deafness he added: *"discharged in December 1952 because of profound deafness which came on shortly after affecting me on early 1949"*.

The Safecracker Provost

Provost Willie Orr spent his political life representing the people of Linwood. He started in 1950 at Renfrew District Council, was elected Provost in 1992, and retired in 1995. However, in his more distant past, during WWII, he played his part in Hitler's downfall by spending the war years as a Safecracker behind enemy lines. He operated throughout Western Europe during the conflict following Allied troops behind enemy lines to blast open safes containing secret documents. He also rubbed shoulders with the notorious safecracker Johnny Ramensky, who didn't always use his talents exclusively for king and country. Provost Orr said: *"During the war it was our job to open safes and get the papers out before they could be destroyed. He [Johnny Ramensky] was promised a free pardon if he did this work for us and that's what he did. But after the war he committed crimes and unfortunately ended up dying in Barlinnie prison. He blew the safe at Linwood Co-op and ended up nearly blowing the roof off. Later-on he visited him at Barlinnie and they had a laugh about it"*

Clydebank Blitz

Linwood folk can remember the windows of houses in the village shaking from the vibrations coming from the bombing blitz on Clydebank, and many watched the action from the tops of the bings.

The following story was submitted to the People's War site by Vijiha Bashir, at BBC Scotland on behalf of Joe Brunetti from Paisley (Contributed on 31 January 2006).

"On the first night of the Clydebank Blitz I was working overtime in Reid Gear Company, Linwood, in Renfrewshire and if I remember correctly the time was around 8 p.m. There was a full moon in a cloudless sky when the bombs started dropping along the Clydeside.

There was an Air raid shelter at the work for all employees, but my friend and I went into the field beside Reid Gear and stood below the thick branches of the trees so that we would not be struck by any shrapnel from the Anti-Aircraft Guns. In the light from the searchlight battery, Inkerman, you could see tracer bullets being fired down the light beam which resulted in one of the searchlights being put out of action.

That night I cycled to my home to Kilbarchan and the journey in the dark was most unpleasant although, happily I arrived home safely. A few days later I cycled to Erskine Ferry and passed a good number of fields where burned-out Incendiary bombs lay. They were white in colour as they were full of Phosphorous and their main function was to cause fires where ever they landed.

I was in my garden, in Kilbarchan, when two land mines were dropped from the German bombers onto Paisley. I saw three flares, which had parachutes attached and these drifted down to ground very slowly and one of the land mines scored a direct hit on a First Aid Post where several of the First Aid Workers were killed instantly. There was a Gas works several hundred yards from where I was standing, and I heard shrapnel falling on to the gas tanks.

One Sunday afternoon the air-raid siren sounded, and a German plane flew over the area, the anti-aircraft guns were firing but they never hit a target. A few nights later the bomber returned, and a bomb was dropped in Kilbarchan. Luckily it landed in a field hurting no one and all you could see was a red glow for a few seconds in the clouds above.

When the Greenock bombing started a few days later I was at that time cycling just outside Kilmacolm, I found a piece of shrapnel on the road and I have it to this day.

I almost forgot to mention the Home Guard of LDV (Local Defence Volunteers). The guards were posted at various sites between towns and villages and I remember one encounter when my friend from Linwood and I were about to cross the 'Shooglie' Bridge at Mill O' Cart when we were stopped by the Home Guard and asked to produce identity cards. The Guard demanded who demanded our card was a well-known Johnstone character by the name of Hector Steel. We said to him "sure you know us", but he wanted the cards just the same. Sadly, he was murdered at the same spot around thirty or forty years later."

Linwood Home Guard

The Home Guard (initially Local Defence Volunteers, or LDV) was an armed citizen militia supporting the British Army during the Second World War. Operational from 1940 to 1944, the Home Guard had 1.5 million local volunteers otherwise ineligible for military service, such as those who were too young or too old to join the regular armed services (regular military service was restricted to those aged 18 to 41) and those in reserved occupations. Their role was to act as a secondary defence force in case of invasion by the forces of Nazi Germany. The Home Guard were to try to slow down the advance of the enemy even by a few hours to give the regular troops time to regroup.

Linwood had its own Platoon, who are pictured and named below.

LINWOOD'S HOME GUARD PLATOON (1940-44)

Back Row: T. McGowan; J. Ritchie; G. Johnston; A. Barr; J. Deighan; T. McCormack; J. Slavin; R. Perrie; J McCurday; T. Carrol; J. McVicar; J. McManus. *2nd Back Row:* W. Marshall; A. Collison; W. Edmiston; W. Hamilton; G. Edmiston; J. Welsh; T. Cassidy; J. McManus; T. Caldwell; J. Anderson; W. Chalmers; W. Watson. *Sitting:* P. Lennon (standing); L/c J. Thomson; Cpl. W. Kerr; Cpl. R. Stevenson; Lieut. A. Eaglesom; Lieut. F. Wilson; M.S.M., Lieut. J. Pinkerton; Sergeant J. Dickson; M.M. Cpl. R. Brown; L/c C. McCurday. *Kneeling:* J. Thomson; A. Eaglesom; Jr., T. McNeil; R. Picken; P. McGivern.

Deafhillock Hostel

Deafhillock Hostel was situated near the corner of Barochan Road and Bridge of Weir Road, just outside Linwood, adjacent to the Deafhillock Roundabout, which was formerly a Toll, or Turnpike, in days gone by. This hostel, like many other around the UK, was set-up in 1941 by Ernest Bevin, the *Minister of Labour and National Service*, as an independent non-profit making organisation to cater for the needs of workers arising out of their employment during the Second World War. In particular, there was difficulty manning the armaments industries because workpeople had to be sent from their homes to places where there was not enough living accommodation, and therefore the government decided to set up hostels in those areas. The Corporation was registered under the *Companies Act 1929* as a company without share capital, within the bounds of ministerial policy and control. Lord Rushcliffe, the former Minister of Labour, was appointed Chairman of the Corporation. By the end of the War, the Corporation was managing 58 industrial hostels and providing over 30,000 places.

After the Second World War, the main function of the Corporation was the provision of accommodation for workers employed away from home on essential reconstruction work. Following a ministerial announcement in November 1954, the hostels programme was reduced, and progressively the remaining hostels were closed. In 1956 the Corporation was wound up.

I was unable to find the exact dates of the opening and closure of the Deafhillock Hostel, but of course would have been between 1941 and 1951 as explained above.

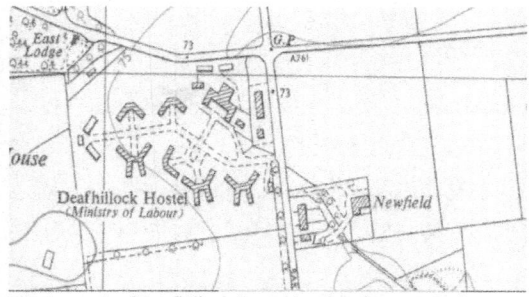
This image is of Deafhillock Hostel is taken from an Ordinance Survey map of the late 1940's.

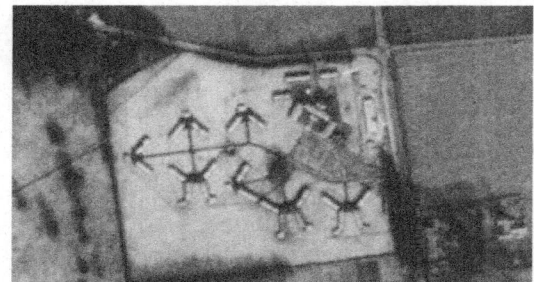
Deafhillock Hostel (ministry of labour) year – 1949. It resembles an airport, or perhaps an alien settlement.

War Memorial Garden

It is hoped, that sometime during the year 2024, that for the first time, there will a War Memorial Garden, obelisk, and wildlife corridor in-place at the entrance to Linwood coming from the Paisley direction, which will be a living memorial for the community.

The Roll of Honour identifies 131 men from Linwood who were killed during war and conflict: 119 Linwood men in the Great War, and 11 in later conflicts.

The Glasgow Invasion & Linwood Expansion

The population of Linwood, which had just been a village from its founding in 1792, grew steadily, but slowly, during the 19th Century thus: (1831) 910, (1841) 1,216, (1861) 1,514, (1871) 1,250, (1881) 1,393. By 1961, some 80 years later, it was still only 2,500, but that was about to change.

In looking at the types of people who came to live and work in Linwood when the car plant opened in 1963, and over the next decade or so, we should first look at their reasons for coming. Many at the time, including government and authorities often referred to them as Glasgow *Overspill*, and because of this local people in Linwood did likewise. However, this was misleading and such a term should never have been used.

The *Collins English Dictionary* states that *overspill* is used to refer to *"people who live near a city because there is no room in the city itself"*. Well, the vast majority of people that came to Linwood did not do so because there was no room in the city of Glasgow, and they were not forced out either. They came simply because the fathers of the families had secured a job at the car plant which guaranteed a house along with their job, so they were not *overspill*. This is backed-up by statistical science.

In the late 1950's and early 1960's, huge new housing estates such as Drumchapel, Easterhouse, and Castlemilk, were built on the outskirts of Glasgow in an effort to tackle Glasgow's desperate post-war housing shortage, as part of *Glasgow Corporation Overspill Policy*. There was 'no room in the city' anymore. Those affected had no choice as their houses were being demolished, and they were not guaranteed jobs with their moves, as those going to Linwood were. Now that - is *overspill* explained, and in action.

In our Facebook Group *'Auld Linwood Town & Surrounds'* (ALTS), we ran a poll asking the question *"How did your family end up in the 'new' [post car plant] Linwood?"*, and provided five options. These options along with the percentage votes were as follows:

1. Dad got house with Job in Car Plant, or other Employer = 48%
2. I'm an Old Villager – was already here before the Influx = 32%
3. Overspill from Glasgow or elsewhere = 13%
4. Moved to a rented house in Linwood = 7%

Note: the population of the group at the time was 2,200 people and the number of respondents was 200, and the vast majority of those polled were born between the 1950' and 1970's.

In analysing the results, we can see that 87% did not consider their families reason for coming to Linwood as being *Overspill*, and nearly half, or 48%, stated that their fathers secured a house with their jobs.

Statistics calculated using the aforementioned figures show that there is just a 6.61% margin of error at a 95% confidence level, that these results are accurate. Therefore, and in conclusion, the long running *Overspill* myth is hereby debunked and substantially proven as such.

Now, in regard to origin of the incomers we ran another poll asking the question *"Of the 48% of Linwood incomers whose fathers got a house with their job, where did your family come to Linwood from?"*

Note: Again, the population of the group at the time was 2,200 people and the number that voted was 200, and the vast majority of those polled were born between the 1950' and 1970's.

The results showed that a massive 96% came from Glasgow districts, 19% of which from Govan district, which represented over 8% of all of the Linwood population today. Springburn district figures were 13%(5.7%), Bridgeton 11%(4.8%), Gorbals 10%(4.4%), and Partick 7%(3.1%). There were thirteen districts of Glasgow represented in the results, as well as Paisley 4%(1.8%)

The incomers to Linwood were offered homes with jobs, most of which were at the Car Plant, although other positions included the likes of Teachers. *Rootes* and *Renfrew County Education Department* advertised homes with jobs.

The village of Linwood grew into a substantial town in less than a decade, as the young workforce was accommodated in local authority housing. There was large-scale migration from Glasgow and other older urban settlements.

Migrants were accommodated in purpose-built local authority housing in Linwood. One incomer stated that *"There was no realistic prospect of obtaining a similar home in Glasgow"*, where he and his wife were starting married life in a rented tenement flat, and he thought, *"a brand-new house, no-one had ever lived in it, and that's for me."*

Only 12% of the workforce was fifty or older, compared with over 25% of the economically active male population of Strathclyde Region as a whole. Seven in ten workers lived in Linwood or neighbouring Paisley and Johnstone, and two in ten travelled daily from Glasgow. In Linwood half the employed population worked for Chrysler, and locals referred to it as *'Rootesville'*, despite the change of ownership in 1967.

Linwood Vast and Rapid Expansion in Housing

With a huge factory that would employee many thousands of workers already being built, it was clear that incoming workers and their families – mainly from Glasgow, would need homes, and very quickly. The SSHA were tasked with building thousands of homes rapidly.

Linwood's population grew rapidly. It grew from 2,500 in 1961, to 10,500 in 1971, then doubled to 23,000 in 1981. Today it is a mere 8,450.

The SSHA had been established in 1937 to provide good-quality social housing. It employed a large team of architects, engineers and quantity surveyors. It was responsible for the construction of post car plant Linwood from early 60's to early 70's. The SSHA had a large Direct Labour Organisation (DLO), a separate unit with its own accounts, and its employees directly employed by Renfrew District Council, who were responsible for construction and maintenance. They helped develop a no-fines concrete building technique which was used to build thousands of houses in Linwood through this period.

The *Scotsman* newspaper reported on the 28th of February 1962 that local authorities have started to build houses for workers at Linwood with nearly the first 300 homes at Linwood itself, now completed, and another 250 are to be begin shortly. There were plans for a further 2,000 by the end of 1963 and, looking much farther ahead, another 3,000 homes are scheduled for the area said the report.

Car Plant owners Roots had been advertising all of the UK for workers for their factory, and the *County of Renfrew Education Committee* advertised for teachers for several schools soon to be built. All of these adverts promised a house with a job.

It was the responsibility of the *Glasgow Overspill Committee* to consider the requirements of such employers and allocate numbers of houses in batches via the SSHA to these skilled workers, who, as mentioned, were not overspill.

Aerial view of the new Linwood in 1963 looking eastwards. The top right-hand quarter shows the already established Linwood with the original village shown in the top right-hand corner. Clippens House and Farm area are on the top left-hand side, and the Combination and Infectious Disease hospital buildings are shown in the bottom middle. The remainder are brand new houses yet to be occupied at this time.

The initial explosion of new houses consisted of the estates between Erskinefauld and Brediland Roads, the houses around Abernethy Drive, the houses around Kintyre Avenue and Cowal Drive, and the houses encapsulated within the looping Stirling Drive area. However, between 1968 and 1972 East Fulton and North Clippens estates would be added. Many of the East Fulton Small Holdings, owned by the *Department of Agriculture and Fisheries*, would need to be demolished for this purpose, but some were taken-over by the SSHA and remain today.

Aerial view from Linwood in 1963 looking west towards Crosslee. Between 1968 and 1971 East Fulton Estate would be built in the area to the mid-left of the photo, and between 169 and 1972 North Clippens Estate would be built in the middle area of the photo - behind where the row of trees is shown.

Teachers Wanted

An advert in the *Scotsman* on the 31st of January 1964 stated that *"only four out of 190 teachers needed for new schools in the Linwood - Johnstone area have been recruited"*, as reported at a meeting of *Renfrewshire Education Committee*. It went on to say that *"the schools are being built to cope with the "bulge" caused by the big influx of labour for the Rootes Hillman motor factory."*

Due to Linwood's very substantial and rapid expansion, with thousands of children coming to live an study, the *County of Renfrew Education Committee* advertised teaching vacancies in the *Scotsman* newspaper during the month of June in various years of the 1960's, just two months before the new schools were scheduled to open, i.e., June 1964 for both St Brendans Primary/High School, and Craigends Primary School; June 1965 for Linwood High School and Mossedge Primary School; June1969 for St Convals and East Fulton Primary Schools. They were looking for teachers of all disciplines for both Non-Denominational and Roman Catholic schools. All adverts promised the provision of houses for successful applicants.

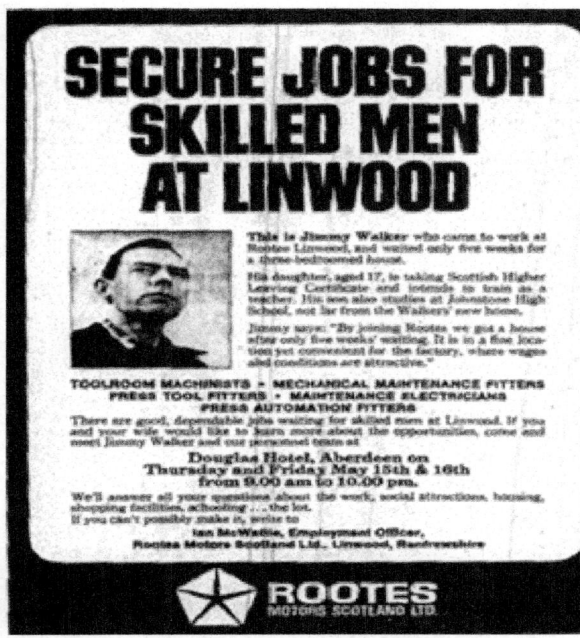

Advertisement in the Aberdeen Evening Express - Tuesday 13th of May 1969. House with job.

The Scotsman - Tuesday 02 December 1959. Houses made available for incoming teachers.

Criticism and Standard of the New Houses

The *Scotsman* newspaper reported on the 05th of February 1963 about a petition protesting against housing conditions at Linwood, which *"was sent yesterday to the director and general manager of Rootes (Scotland) Ltd., Mr W. F. C. Bryant, by 16 wives of junior executives of the firm. The women moved in the previous autumn to houses classified as executive type four apartments"* One wife complained that one of her apartments was no bigger than a box-room and another complained of the view in that all they could see was the "rusty tin huts" across the road."

It is likely the houses they were complaining about were those located Muirhead Drive overlooking the old Combination Isolation Hospital. They were also unhappy at the conditions of roads and footpaths saying that they were unsatisfactory - the shops being *"too far away"*, and that there are not enough of them. The rent of the Rootes four-apartment house at this time was set at £10 a month, plus 35s for a lock-up garage.

The *Scotsman* again reported on the 06th of May, 1963, on the standard of the housing by referring to a double-page article in yesterday's *Sunday Times* colour magazine which criticised the building and planning of the new town of Linwood growing around the Rootes Hillman factory opened last week, and claimed that *"instead of being Scotland's pride which it could have been — it had become a miniature Dagenham 'north of the border'."* The writer said that *"the houses and blocks of flat in concrete and pebble-dash could not even be called uniform in their ugliness"*. Although tenants said that Linwood was better than Glasgow, he asked: *"but is better than Glasgow good enough? Will not a drab, ill-planned housing development such as Linwood become, in time, almost as dismal as the dank tenements of the city?"* Renfrew County Council engineer and planning officer, Mr Andrew Wilson, said in defence of the new houses *"that the article portrayed present conditions, and not what the town would be like when development, including beautification, was completed."* The county had been asked by the *Secretary of State for Scotland* to carry out a crash programme —*"our first task was to build quickly and get the factory started"* — and this had been done with 300 houses completed in 35 weeks."

Executives' wives and a distant English reporters views are one thing, but as one of those who grew new in a brand new four-apartment SSHA house in Linwood, I know that we all thought that the SSHA houses were great. They were new, clean, roomy, and many had gardens and their own parking space. They had instant hot water, baths, lofts for storage space. Most of us didn't know any better, but those who did remember the tenements of Glasgow thought they were moving into a palace in the countryside.

Notable People & Characters
Private Hugh McIver VC MM*

Hugh McIver (1890-1918) was born on 21st June 1890 at No. 30 Napier Street, Linwood, to Hugh and Mary McIver (nee Flynn) a Scottish Roman Catholic couple who were descended from Irish immigrants. Hugh was the second oldest of Hugh and Mary McIver's seven surviving children, and like his father before him Hugh would become a coal miner. At the age of 4 years of age Hugh's family moved to Newton, Lanarkshire, part of the parish of Cambuslang, as he spent the majority of his life living and working in Newton.

Hugh went to work in the mines with the *Messrs James Dunlop & Co.*, Newton No. 1 Colliery, Cambuslang, when he was just 14. Ironically, a company that also operated next to Napier Street where he was born.

Hugh joined the special reserve of the *Highland Light Infantry* (HLI) on 26th March 1914, less than five months before the outbreak of the First World War, pledging to remain in the reserve for six years' service. Having attested into the reserve of the HLI, however, he was discharged 55 days later on 19th May 1914. Private McIver's character is stated quite simply as 'BAD'. He was formally discharged as he was deemed 'not likely to become an efficient Special Reservist'. To those of us who know how this story ends, it is impossible not to possess a wry smile as we think of the decorated soldier Hugh would so soon become.

On the outbreak of war less than six months later, Hugh enlisted with the *Royal Scots* on 18th August 1914 the Glencorse Barracks and was sent to the Western Front.

The 5ft 4½ inch 9½ stone Private McIver had spent over two years on the Western Front and had been wounded having previously received treatment for myalgia and rheumatism. He had also appeared in the London Gazette on 21st September 1916 to note the award of his first Military Medal, the second highest award for bravery in the ranks.

On 15th July 1918 an entry in the War Diary states that *"daylight patrols were successful in capturing four of the enemy. This patrol consisted of 4 other ranks under 2/Lieut HM Somerville'. Just 12 days later, an entry in the battalion War Diary informs us that 'the following awards were granted for "daring" and initiative during daylight patrols in the enemy lines on 15th July...'. One of the awards was a 'Bar to Military Medal...[for]Private H McIver (12311) MM of "C" Coy 2nd Battalion Royal Scots".

One month later the *2nd Battalion Royal Scots* were involved in a significant attack at Courcelles-le-Comte that started on 21st August 1918, and severe fighting with the enemy continued until 25th August when the men are recorded as 'resting and clearing up'. On 23rd August 1918 east of Courcelle-le Compte, France, Private McIver was employed as a company-runner and under heavy artillery and machine-gun fire carried messages regardless of his own safety. Single-handed he pursued an enemy scout into a machine-gun post and having killed six of the garrison, captured 20 prisoners and two machine-guns. Later he succeeded, at great personal risk, in stopping the fire of a British tank which was directed in error against our own troops.

Nine days after Hugh was involved in the above act of gallantry, he was killed in action on 2nd September 1918 during an attack near the village of Noreuil. The War Diary indicates that Private McIver's company were further advancing up a trench when they were *"held up by machine gun fire"*. It is at this time that it appears Hugh was killed. The document further notes that two Lieutenants and 24 other ranks of the *Royal Scots* were also killed on 2nd September, while a further six men were recorded as missing.

Hugh was buried in Vraucourt Copse Cemetery with full military honours. On 13th February 1919, his parents travelled from Scotland to Buckingham Palace to receive his VC from King George V. Tragically, less than a month later, Hugh's father would be killed in an accident in the pits. His medals including the VC, MM and Bar, 1914-15 Star, British War Medal 1914-20 and Victory Medal 1914-19 are now held by the *Royal Scots Greys Museum* in Edinburgh Castle. They purchased the medals in 1974.

In 2015, Kier Homes named a street in their Hawkhead Village development in Paisley, Hugh McIver Avenue, in memory of him. In 2018 his home town of Linwood unveiled a commemorative plaque outside the Tweedie Hall.

I don't think I've ever learned of such acts of heroism, not even in a make-believe Hollywood movie. Audie Murphy couldn't lace his boots.

Private Hugh McIver VC MM*, is undoubtably the greatest ever person to be born in Linwood.

Private Hugh McIver VC MM* - Napier Street born.

Jessie Leitch sitting in the Harper family's garden - circa 1920's.

'Andy Broke' – so called because he called out "Aanee Broke".

Dugald Semple – 'The Hermit of Linwood Moss'. Relaxed at the door of his 'wheelhouse' at Linwood Moss in 1907 during the period he was working as a draughtsman.

Miss Jessie Wills Leitch was a *Titanic* survivor, who was born in Linwood, Renfrewshire, Scotland on the 08th of November 1880. Her father John Leitch was also a native of Linwood whilst her mother Jessie Gillespie Bell was from Govan, Lanarkshire. Jessie boarded the *Titanic* ship with her husband Paster John Harper and his daughter Nana on the 10th of April 1912 at Southampton as second-class passengers, as they were travelling to a church in Chicago, Illinois.

The following is Jessie's account of that night.

John Harper has told Jessie about midnight that the vessel had struck an iceberg. While she was dressing when he went to learn further particulars and returned to say that the order had been given to put on the life belts. Jessie did so, and, picking up Nana in his arms, he took her up to the deck. There the women were ordered to the upperdeck. She had to climb a vertical iron ladder and John Harper brought Nana after her up the ladder and the men at the top lifted Nana up to me Jessie again. There was no opportunity for any farewell, and, in fact, even then they did not realise the danger, as they were assured again and again that the vessel could not sink, and that the *Olympic* vessel would be alongside at any minute, and that the women and children were to be put into the boats first and the men to follow, and that there were boats sufficient for all. Their boat was well manned; it was the eleventh to leave the vessel. After about half an hour the *Titanic* went down when they were about a mile away.

Jessie re-married and later died in the *War Memorial Hospital* in Llanidloes, Wales, on 6 February 1963 aged 82.

Linwood has another link with the Titanic disaster. 19-year-old James Blackie was from Paisley, but worked in Linwood as a Signwriter. He was emigrating and had set sale for the other side of the Atlantic to start a new life, but perished when the ship sank after hitting an iceberg. His family were only compensated £115 for the young man's life, which was reduced to a meagre £90 once legal expenses had been paid.

Andy Broke

This character walked around the streets of Linwood in the early 1020's shouting "Aanee Broke" in his thick Irish accent. He was collecting kitchen waste, like potato and vegetable peelings to feds his pigs at his Piggery located somewhere around Linwood Moss and Georgetown area. When the children took out waste to him, they were rewarded with a bit of a bit of home-made "glassy toffee". However, most mothers told their children not to eat the toffee, but of course, that instruction only made it more attractive. Andy's visits didn't last very long and within a couple of years his call was no longer heard as his visits had ceased for some reason.

Dugald Semple (The Hermit of Linwood Moss)

Dugald Semple was a controversial figure in his day. He was a co-founder of the *Vegan Society* in 1944 but had been a vegan long before the term was coined, and was an advocate of simple, healthy, open-air living.

He was born in Johnstone, where he lived with his family on Johnstone High Street. In his teens Dugald became a vegetarian, which was a heresy to his parents, who were staunch Calvinistic. It was tantamount to a criticism of Jesus who told his disciples where to fish and of the apostles Peter, Andrew, James, and John who were fishermen His mother accused him of being devil-possessed.

He then won a bursary to Paisley Grammar School and served an apprenticeship as an engineering draughtsman in a machine tool shop in Linwood where he earned 10s a week, and through camping during his summer holidays had a longing for freedom and a more natural mode of living. It seemed to him that so-called civilization was all wrong which compelled folks to work so hard most of the year that they could only get a few weeks' rest at Fair-time. It was "getting a living", not "living".

In 1907, he moved into a tent, and later an old omnibus located on Linwood Moss. He said:

"After a short stay at the Moss, I was in love with the open-air life, even though it was mostly during weekends. The birds were such friendly companions, and I believe the rabbits thought I was playing at a "wee hoose" But of dear! the crowds which came to see me on Sundays were no small problem, especially after the newspapers sent thousands to see The Hermit of Linwood Moss'. Truly, it was most embarrassing, especially as I was still following my occupation as usual. Unfortunately, the crowds caused my removal to Bridge of Weir, where I camped on the banks of the River Gryfe."

A regular visitor to Ailsa Craig, he was known locally as the 'Bird Man' and was an enthusiast for outdoor living, publishing a book entitled *A Free Man's Philosophy*. He welcomed walkers and cyclists who often camped on his land.

In 1916, he was a conscientious objector and thus exempted from military service on condition that he continued lecturing on food economy. He regularly appeared on radio programmes, including *Out with Romany and Hutman* of the BBC. He lived with his wife Cathie in London for two years when he was secretary of the *Vegetarian Society*.

In 1963, Dugald detailed his dietary journey:

"I began rather drastically in 1910 by cutting out not only all meat or flesh foods, but milk, eggs, butter, tea and coffee. Cheese I have never eaten; indeed, I hate the very smell of this decayed milk. Next, I adopted a diet of nuts, fruit, cereals and vegetables. On this Edenic fare I lived for some ten years, and found that my health and strength were greatly improved. While I was in London (during WWI), I found it necessary to add some dairy products to my meals, but on returning to Scotland I gradually eliminated these again."

In later years, Semple did speaking tours of the USA, Canada, India and Europe to promote his best-selling lifestyle books. He became Vice-President of the *International Vegan Union* and the *World Vegetarian Congress*, and Honorary President of the *Scottish Vegetarian Society*.

Like many Scots, Semple is celebrated more abroad than at home. At one point, he could count Indian leader Mahatma Ghandi, who he met in London in 1931, as a close friend. In his time, he was very well known, both in Scotland and abroad, but has been largely forgotten in recent years. In later life, he lived in a modern cottage and even owned a car. Dugald Semple died in a nursing home in Fairlie, aged 79.

Dominic Di Ciacca was a big-hearted owner of two fish and chip shops in Linwood who dedicated more than forty years of his life to helping others in the town. Family man Domenic was born in the village of La Rocca in Italy in 1936 and followed his older brother Onorios to Scotland in 1956, marrying Anna (known as Nina) in 1960. He had initially worked on a farm in Kilbirnie and in a café before coming to Linwood, where he became well known after opening the town's first fish and chip shop in Bridge Street in the early 1960's, having converted the old post office building. And through the years so many people worked for him in his shops at some point, especially youngsters.

Dominic was a central part of the community in Linwood, often asking his customers how they and their families were getting on. He sponsored the local boxing club and helped pay for some of the equipment, regularly gave money to help a local school football team, and he even provided food for folks at the time of a funeral.

Domenic Di Ciacca sadly passed away aged 73 at the Royal Alexandra Hospital after suffering from with motor neurone disease.

Dr Agnes Malcolm

Dr Agnes Malcolm - quite simply a doctor like no other, a doctor that went way beyond the call of duty, and a doctor that really cared for the people she attended to.

In our Facebook Group *'Auld Linwood Town & Surrounds' (ALTS)*, I asked the members in a Poll, *"of all the Linwood people of the past that we knew of, who would be most deserving of being awarded an O.B.E."* The winner with an overwhelming 65% was Dr Agnes Malcolm, 43% ahead of the second placed person.

My own first memory of her was when I was only four or five years old, and I was taken to see her by my mum in the 'old wooden hut' practice at near the corner of what was once Linwood Cross. Even at this age I could see that she had a very pleasant disposition. And it was the same when I visited her many times over the years in the new Clinic, from when she moved there in December 1971

Dr Malcolm never married and lived with her sister in the nearby village of Brookfield, who also never married. Her brother, Donald Malcolm, owner of the road haulage firm, also lived nearby in the village. My friends and I would go to

Brookfield to steal fruit from trees in the rich people gardens, but when we went to her house, she just told us *"no need to steal boys, just chap my door and I'll give you my windfalls"*, and she'd take us into her house and give us a drink of diluting orange and a polly-bag for the windfalls we'd gather. This taught us a valuable lesson in life and I couldn't help but think that she was the most sincerest human being I'd ever met, then, and since

Many ALTS members relate that Dr Malcom delivered them in their houses, and many remember the lady, who you could sit and have a chat and a *fag* with, in her surgery. Below I have listed a few of the anecdotes that members of ALTS have related to me.

Jane McIlveen: *"I remember having croup, it was around 1969. I must have been about five and Dr Malcolm came out in the middle of the night to sit with me as I was lying on the couch with a kettle boiling beside me, and my mum at my side. I've seen my own have croup and know how scary it is to watch, so thank you Dr Malcolm for being there with my mum when we both needed you".*

Tommy Grant: *"Dr Malcolm was an absolute angel and definitely the friend of Car Plant workers with her sick notes at appropriate" times".*

Michael Mullen: *"When Dr Malcolm retired, she did Counselling Bereavement, Depression etc, House calls – mostly. I remember one day she drove into Montrose Place around 1995 as I was coming out my dad's house at No2. I said "are you Dr Malcolm" and she smiled and said "yes, you've got a good memory young man". "I told her she delivered me in our house in 1964. She paused and looked at me and said "let me think, is your surname McMillan?". I said no, it's Mullen. "Aw son my memories not as good as it used to be" she replied, smiled went away and chapped someone's door. What a Lady!"*

Diane Speirs Wright: *"I suffered from bad asthma as a kid and she came out all times of the night and stayed with me. Just spoke to my mum about Dr Malcolm and she said she was a one of a kind and knew everyone in Linwood. She drove through Linwood waving at everyone like she was the Queen. She came to my house immediately day or night and followed up the next day after I was blue lighted to the hospital a few times by chapping the door the next morning to find out how I was. This was despite the fact she had been up late the night before with the call out."*

Betsy Brennan: *"Dr Malcolm came from Dr Carrick's Surgery in Johnstone in the 1960's, to open her Surgery in Linwood. Due to kidney issues, I was never away from her Surgery, where we enjoyed a good-few cigarettes together. I remember once spraining my ankle badly; she said to use a plastic bag like a sock on it, and it worked. She was a brilliant Doctor."*

Diane Nisbett: *"She had a drawer full of chocolate for the weans who were scared of doctors, and it worked a treat."*

Extraordinary Linwood Stories
Raising the Dead

The *Paisley and Renfrewshire Advertiser* reported on the 1st of April 1865 of the strange of the Linwood woman whose body was exhumed due to suspected foul play. Yet, despite this significant date, the story was true.

The unnamed woman, the wife of a miner at Linwood, had been interred in the Paisley West-end the previous Monday, but was to be exhumed, fur the purpose of undergoing a *post-mortem* examination, to ascertain whether the deceased had died from the effects of poison, which had been wilfully administered.

It appeared that some friends of the woman had presented petition to the Renfrew County Fiscal, expressing suspicion that her death was the result of foul play, and desiring that the body might be exhumed and examined. A warrant for this purpose was accordingly granted, and about seven o'clock on Thursday morning Dr McKinlay, who was assisted by Dr Richmond, proceeded to the cemetery, and had the body taken from the grave. It was conveyed to one of the tool sheds, where it was carefully inspected by the medical gentlemen, and the result, understand, left not the slightest doubt that the woman had died from natural causes.

During the investigation a large crowd had gathered outside the cemetery gate, which was shut to keep the people from entering, and the most absurd suspicions and innuendos were indulged in until after the examination, when the crowd gradually dispersed. Like many popular rumours, the story turned out to be utterly groundless. The husband of the deceased is well-doing working man, and he was never known to have treated his wife harshly. The result of the post-mortem examination was reported to the Crown authorities as per usual in such cases.

The Extraordinary Adventure of Two Miners on a Spree.

The *Renfrewshire Independent* reported on the 25th of November 1871, of an extraordinary, but amusing story, of two miners from Beith.

The miners had hired a dog-cart to take them to Howwood for the purpose of 'having a spree.' The dog-cart belonged to Mr Wilson of the Saracen's Inn, Beith, and the horse was the property of another party. One of the miners was lame and used a crutch.

After enjoying themselves at Howwood till a late hour, they headed for home, drunk and falling asleep, and as a result of this the horse wandered in the opposite direction. The one with the crutch had lain down in the dog-cart, whilst the other, though sleeping, kept his seat.

The horse must have travelled through Johnstone, and passed through Deafhillock toll, turning right on Bridge of Weir Road and soon reaching the toll at Clippens Road, near Linwood, when it turned to the right, and took the read leading to the Mill O'Cart Farm, occupied by Mr McDougall. Here the miners' adventurers were doomed to meet with a somewhat disagreeable check to their progress; for the one who was sleeping soundly in the bottom of the dog-cart awoke, believing that he had now arrived safely at Beith, but he had scarcely turned to speak to his companion when both were immersed over their heads in water, the horse having walked straight into the River Black Cart.

The river was at this time swollen to a great extent by the recent rains. The men struggled in the water for some time and the able bodied one seems to have gotten ashore first, and as the dog-cart had capsized, the disabled one got his head above the water and got a hold of one of the wheels, to which he gripped with immovable tenacity. The one who got out safely sought help, but found this difficult as he had no idea where he was, nor did he know what direction to take. As the farmer's dog was barking and making a great noise, he went straight in the direction of the dog, believing that there must be some human habitation not far off. But amazingly his calamitous luck continued when he soon plunged over the head in the nearby Mill Lade, which was nine feet deep at this location, and as he couldn't swim, he must have thought that he'd soon perish. But he got bold of some bushes at the edge of the Lade, he managed, however, to get out of the water for the second time, but was much exhausted.

In the meantime, his companion, with much difficulty, bad succeeded in reaching dry land; but as he had lost his crutch his powers of locomotion were very much curtailed, and he had to creep on his bands. He crawled to the door of the farm house, where shouted waken the inhabitants; but as the dog, who got to within a few feet of him, made a spring now and then to catch him, he howled-out *"Murder"* being uncertain whether he would be drowned or mauled. The now awakened farmer, armed himself with a huge cudgel to repel the invaders. The two men by this time had become considerably sober, and their sufferings from cold and exposure were great.

Shouting at the door for admittance, the crutchless miner was crying *"Oh, let me in, or I'll dee! Oh mistress, if you had a heart as saft's a whinstane you would let me in. I've nae legs, an' am perished' o' cauld."*

When the farmer opened the door, the stranger collapsed helpless at his feet, completely exhausted. His partner soon joined him there, and on their situation being ascertained by the farmer a large fire was kindled in the kitchen, their wet clothes taken off and dried, and a clean shirt, and other clothes given to each of them. Both tea and whisky were also given them, and they were otherwise treated with the greatest hospitality.

About seven o'clock the next morning a number of miners who were passing, by the assistance of ropes got the horse and dog-cart out of the water, the horse being drowned; and thus ended one of the most miraculous escapes from death ever recorded.

The Tragedy of the Late Rev. William Milne

The *Paisley & Renfrewshire Gazette* reported on 12th of January 1884, the tragedy that became Linwood's Parish Minister, the Rev. William Milne. The story had been recounted to the congregation at the end of a church service by his successor, the Rev. J. A. Abernethy.

On Christmas Day, Mr Milne went on horseback to visit an aged minister who was dying, and some miles from the Manse be met a cart loaded with wood, when, as his horse became restive and shy, he drew up to the roadside to allow the cart to pass. His horse then reared and fell with him into a ditch, and, in the effort to rise, rolled over and broke his arm and leg, and also, it is thought, caused him some internal injury.

When Mr. Milne got home and his injuries had been attended to, the doctor thought that there was nothing to suggest a fatal issue, and in a day or two gave him strong hopes of a complete recovery.

Mr. Milne was quite cheerful, and on Saturday dictated an intimation to a brother minister to be read from the pulpit next day concerning an assistant for the work during his confinement. On Sunday he was still cheerful, and talked hopefully to his wife, the doctor, and the minister who preached for him that day, and partook of a hearty dinner; but while the rest of the household were dining, they heard a cry, and, hastening to his room, found him in the throes of death. He motioned to Mrs. Milne as if to speak to her, but, before he could utter a word, he was dead.

The Rev. J. A. Abernethy summed-up by saying *"Many could be better spared, we think, in view of such a death; but God's ways are not as oar ways, nor His thoughts as our thoughts, and he giveth his beloved sleep."*

Mr. Milne had laboured for served for seven years in this new Parish, which he was responsible for setting-up.

The Miracles of the Scottish Lourdes for Redan Rows Residents.

The *Sunday Post* reported on the 15th of July 1923 of miraculous events in the village of Linwood. Their correspondent visited a community there known has Redan Rows, which were four rows of former single-storey miner cottages, and also the nearby Napier Street.

The correspondent was there to interview residents who had apparently been cured after a visit of a charabanc party to the Grotto at Carfin, and it seems that no less than four persons have been cured of their ills.

An old woman called Mrs Gillespie of 28 Redan Rows, was seated, and told that she had been going about the village for twelve years or so with the aid of crutch and a stick due to the sinews her leg had been cut. She said *"I am cured, thank God. Wait and I'll show you how I can walk,"* and with that she joyfully rose to her feet and paced the kitchen floor. She went on *"I knew before went last Sunday I would get better,"* she said, and *"since then I have been walking every day with more ease. I am seventy-two years of age."*

Then there was a little girl named Isa Fern, living in Napier Street, who had been deaf and dumb from her early childhood. Her mother said that Isa (14) had fallen downstairs when a child of one year and eight months, and since then she had been unable to speak or hear. Mrs Fern explained that, along with thirty others and herself, Isa had journeyed to Carfin the previous Sunday. They had just left the Grotto when a bell tolled, and the girl, turning to her mother, asked, *"do you hear the chapel bell?"*.

In speaking with the little girl for a minute two, the correspondent noticed that there was hesitancy in her replies, this thought this natural under the circumstances, for it had to be borne in mind that it was as a baby that she last spoke.

Mrs Fern stated that daily since Sunday her daughter's speech had been improving, and her hearing gradually becoming more acute.

Mrs Fern then related to the correspondent the other two cures - that of an old man, Michael Boyle, and a boy, James McGovern, both residing in Napier Street also.

In the case of Mr Boyle, has been unable to dress himself for a long time back owing to a stiffening of the joints following rheumatics, but it has been found that since his return from the Grotto at Carfin he can put on and discard his own clothes as in his younger days, before his infirmity.

And then there was the case of the boy McGovern, who was away on holiday at the time, but he was said to be suffering from a tubercular knee, and walked with a pronounced lameness, which precluded him from joining with his mates in their robust play. He was now, however, as agile as the others.

The four cures were much discussed throughout the village, and another charabanc load was due to leave this same day, to see the famous Grotto.

REFERENCES AND THANKS
References
Books
Linwood, Paisley and District (1953), by the Reverend John C. Hill
Linwood (Images of Scotland), (1999), by James Winters
The Irish in Britain, (1894), by John Denvir
The Industries of Scotland: Their Rise, Progress and Present Condition, (1869), by David Bremner

Websites
The National Archives of Scotland
The National Library of Scotland
National Collection of Aerial Photography
Canmore: National Record of the Historic Environment
British Newspaper Archive
Renfrewshire Local History Forum
Watson's Paisley & District Directory
Historic Environment Scotland

Newspapers
Paisley & Renfrewshire Gazette
Renfrewshire Independent
The Paisley Daily Express
The Paisley Herald & Renfrewshire Advertiser
The Glasgow Herald
Glasgow Citizen
Glasgow Chronicle
Glasgow Weekly Mail
Glasgow Free Press
The Glasgow Observer and Catholic Herald
The Daily Record
The Sunday Mail
The Scotsman
Sunday Post
Caledonian Mercury
Edinburgh Gazette
Greenock Telegraph & Clyde Shipping Gazette
Dundee Evening Telegraph
Dundee Courier
Aberdeen Press and Journal
North British Daily Mail
Carlisle Journal
Liverpool Echo
Birmingham Daily Post
Coventry Evening Telegraph
Central Somerset Gazette

Other Sources
PhD Thesis: Examining the 'Hard-Boiled Bunch': Work Culture and Industrial Relations at The Linwood Car Plant, c. 1963-1981, by Alison Julia Gilmour (2010)
Royal Ordinance Survey Book [Vol. 14]
BBC Scotland
Various accounts, documents and photos provided by the members of *Auld Linwood Town & Surrounds* Facebook group.

Thanks
The members of *Auld Linwood Town & Surrounds* Facebook group.
Sisters Betsy Brennan and Donna Scott
Others as mentioned throughout the book for their contributions